SNAPSHOTS

SNAPSHOTS

A Kaleidoscope of Human Experience
through Poetry and Short Stories

LISA BRUENS

Published by Lisa Bruens
lisabruens88@gmail.com

First published 2024

Copyright © Lisa Bruens, 2024

The moral right of the author has been asserted.

All rights reserved. Without limiting the rights under copyright restricted above, no part of this publication may be reproduced, stored in or introduced into a retrieval system, or transmitted, in any form or by any means (electronic, mechanical, photocopying, recording or otherwise), without the prior written permission of the copyright owner and publisher of this book.

Disclaimer: The content of this book is a mix of fiction and nonfiction, as perceived by the author's expanding life experience. There is no intent whatsoever, to judge or blame anyone mentioned. The author and publisher claim no responsibility to any reader, or any person mentioned, for any liability, loss or alleged reaction to the interpretation of the material in this book.

 A catalogue record for this book is available from the National Library of Australia

ISBN 978 0 6486253 0 8 (pbk)

Designed and typeset by Helen Christie, Blue Wren Books
Cover image by iStock.com/Naqiewi
Author photo by Josh Symons
Printed and bound by Ingram Spark

I dedicate this book to my fellow humans
who are beginning to remember the Truth that
only LOVE is real.

FOREWORD

Snapshot: (Noun) *An informal photograph taken quickly, typically with a small handheld camera.*

You are aware all through this book that this is cinema verite, handheld, vulnerable, real, and at times shaky under the weight of the message. But like all edgy exposés it is fuelled by passion, and, 'A take me as I am, or fuck off attitude.'

Lisa sets the tone with her first poem, 'Ask me no Questions and I'll tell you no Lies'. Her approach is brazen, honest and at times, searingly conspiratorial as she leads us on her personal journey of responses to the contemporary socio-political landscape; she points to where we stand idly by, mute, in the face of the degradation of our own humanity. Thank God for observers like Lisa Bruens who feel deeply about what is happening, and are able to plumb the depths synthesising and crystallising the zeitgeist into poignant and potent pieces of writing. Her motive is to share and offer insight from her own life. I really enjoyed reading this book. I saw a lot of my own concerns affirmed in her writing. The poems are real, and her voice authentic. It is like she is sitting beside me talking a strange and simple poetry with a voice my heart responds to.

In my work as a facilitator, and community creator, I am vitally interested in the new narratives that give meaning to contemporary life. We are in need of new narratives to lead us and feed us with meaning. We are seeking fulfilment in deeper places now. In a world that is fraying at its edges, new voices will surface and be heard. There will no longer be the single voice crying from the wilderness, for we are all in the new wilderness, not lost but learning. A tribe of voices will be heard. We are leaving the land of celebrity and returning to the small honest voice of our fellow travellers. We will learn from one another, a pastiche of learning, as opposed to academic manual.

There will be many and we will receive succour and inspiration from their soul searching. These new leaders are showing themselves across a variety of disciplines and formats. There is a converging of business, social change, arts, human behaviour and spirituality. This new territory belongs to the brave.

I am fascinated by people with the courage to follow their highest calling, choosing to lead from the fringes, and to live lives of meaning and depth. They seek wisdom over riches, happily many find both! Lisa's book is a wonderful example of this, and a salient reminder that owning your uniqueness, and sharing it with others is such a great gift.

This book is written in an easy uncomplicated language. Tender poems, cheeky, insightful short stories, articles and opinion pieces combine into a kaleidoscope of insight, and feeling, which evoke both discomfort and hope. She writes across a broad range of issues calling upon us to return to a deeper sense of humanity. Her stories sculpt fragmented moments into poignant stories, all too familiar, and sad.

Lisa writes about a world in deep change. She points to where the underbelly of corporate greed, media manipulation and failing governmental policies are now seen for what they are, and where spin was once the currency of the day, people are waking up. At the edges she suggests nothing has changed since Nero fiddled, with Rome as his flaming backdrop; uncomfortable truths, unmasked. Scary topics: chem trails, crooked business, murky religion, smoke and mirrors media, and then small snippets of romance, hope and sadness, the human side of life, broken bones, lost love, facts and figures all get an airing. Snapshots of modern life through the eyes of a writer brave enough to tell us: the emperor has no clothes on.

There is something hopeful and haunting at the core of her writing. She sees the magnificence of humanity, and how that is degraded. Her tone is hopeful, and we are reminded of the power of inner wisdom, her observations are a clarion call for us to return to the power of love within.

There is hope in these pages. Lisa humanises the modern journey, and offers a reminder to hold firm to deeper values. Give yourself time and space to meander through this book poem by poem, story by story, savouring and honouring the journey of a soulful traveller. This is a labour of love with a value way beyond its words.

Julian Noel
Founder of Shine Global,
a global community of change makers
shineglobal.com.au

CONTENTS

Preface   *xiii*
Acknowledgements   *xv*

Introduction   1

POETRY
Ask me no Questions and I'll tell you no Lies (2013)   7
My Red Gum Friend (2013)   9
Do me no Favours (2013)   11
Pull Your Finger Out! (2013)   14
Weeping Tigers (2012)   17
A Plea for Help (2023)   20
Father my Father (1997)   21
The Affluent Society (2013)   23
Boys in Blue (2012)   26
The Beginning of the End (2012)   28
The Pot of Gold (1996)   30
Step Up (2012)   31
Still Dithering (2012)   33
I Wouldn't be a Woman for Quids (2012)   35
A Memory (4a Wilkinson Street) (2012)   37
When I Stopped Running (2012)   38
My Christmas Wish (2012)   40
Ascension (2022)   42

SHORT STORIES
I Was There! (2012)   47
Lily the Barmaid (2013)   50
Sitting on the Esky (2012)   56
There is Something I Must Tell You (2012)   59
Checkmate (2012)   62

Stage Interlude (2012)	66
Turning Loneliness into Solitude (2013)	70
Hand to Mouth (2013)	74
Cough in your Elbow (2022)	78
Shock Treatment (2012)	80
Why I don't want to be Prime Minister (2012)	84
Rough Justice (2012)	88
The Dance of Spring (2013)	92
Feel the Burn (2013)	94
The Lawn Chair (2012)	97
The Time Traveller (2012)	101

TEN-MINUTE TOPICS

The Bear is Growling	109
Elegant Restraint	110
Lexicography, Cough, Sigh, Alphabet, Multiply, Lunch, Cats Litter, Batter, Cloth	111
The Sandman	112
Bells and Whistles	113
The Comeback	114
Retirement	115
Notes	117

PREFACE

The human experience is wide and varied and comes in different shapes, sizes, colours, skills, strengths, weaknesses … and yet we nearly all believe in some way, that we are separate from LOVE (God, Source, …), that we are unworthy, even sinful, and that God has forgotten us down here on earth.

Collective themes from childhood conditioning and experiences such as 'not good enough', 'unworthy', 'unlovable', 'abandoned', have become unconscious mentors for many and shaped not only our own lives, but the world in which we live.

I remember being a naïve, wide-eyed child who had her dreams of how she thought her life would unfold. As the years rolled by something else seemed to be in charge and the yellow brick road of my wistful imagination remained an unrealised dream.

I wrote my first poem when I was eight years old. I can still remember sitting at the back booth of my parent's Eldorado Milk Bar in Kaitaia, New Zealand, and writing a poem about 'The mini car,' our family car at the time. As I grew older, writing became something I did to express myself.

During my thirties, I began to sporadically journal thoughts and ideas that I felt needed recording. I had an idea at the back of my mind that one day I would publish a book. As time went by and life continued, I noticed that a poem or short story often came into being at the end of a growth experience.

One day as I was driving along the road, I heard the words 'It's time,' and I knew in that instant that my book was ready to be born.

In *Snapshots* I offer you a kaleidoscope of human experience, as seen through my eyes. I trust that you will find something to warm your heart, something to give you hope, and something to give you inspiration as we navigate our way through a challenging and changing world.

ACKNOWLEDGEMENTS

I would like to thank the conveners of the Blaxland (NSW, Australia) U3A Writing Group—Christine Hayes and Warren Nicholls—for your commitment, your feedback and your support, and to the U3A Writing Group of 2012 and 2013, for listening to me as I built my confidence and shared my sometimes challenging pieces.

Thank you to Cathy Lamond, David Tobin, Denise Sirol, and Daphne Knox, for reading my creations and getting me started.

Thank you to David, Denise and Christine, for your initial editorial support and your feedback, and to Veronica Scarrow for motivating me to finally manifest my book.

Thank you to Julian Noel—founder of Shine Global—for your inspiring Foreword, and for the wonderful work you do for humanity.

Thank you to my son Josh Symons for the back page photo.

Thank you to Helen Christie from Blue Wren Books, for creating my lovely book cover, and getting my book ready for publishing.

Love, Peace and Gratitude to all of my family,
To all of my friends,
To all of my fellow humans that I have met along the way,
and To all of my fellow humans that I have yet to meet!

INTRODUCTION

Snapshots, is a collection of poems and short stories I wrote from 1991 to 2023, most of which were written from February 2012 to mid-2013 when I attended a weekly U3A Creative Writing group in Blaxland, Blue Mountains, Australia.

At the end of each session we were given three titles to take away with us. Our homework was to choose one title and write something for our next meeting. I quickly discovered that beginning my poems and short stories with a title, provided a focal point for something to be gestated and birthed. Sometimes the labour was short indeed, and the words downloaded quickly. Other times it felt like I needed a forceps delivery because the 'child' was a bit stuck. Then there were those occasions when I felt sure that I needed a caesarean, as the 'child' appeared to have changed its mind and didn't want to engage at all!!!

Like being at the birth of a new born child and holding that child for the very first time, it can be an interesting experience to hold that written creation when you feel like there is nothing else you can add to it.

Some of the poems and stories in this book are complete fiction, and some are autobiographical. The rest are varying blends of fact and fiction. Together they are a kaleidoscope of human experience, a collection of snapshots of the world in which I live.

As I have watched the distance between my birth and 'this moment' increase with time and take me beyond my mid years, I have seen changes that I wouldn't, and couldn't, have considered as a young person.

The decades continue to pass, fads come and go. Music and fashion change and 'evolve', then recycle for a retro phase. Celebrities rise, and some fall. The dance of Politics takes a jump to the left then a shimmy to the right. Friends come and go. Wars are still threatening and killing.

The meaning of life takes on many guises, depending on who is seeking and what their values are. In 1969, the Woodstock Festival was held in Ulster County, New York State, USA. I was a young eleven-year-old Aquarian living in Kaitaia, New Zealand, but my heart and soul could feel the promise of a collective desire for true peace and change. The Peace Movement had been around for a few years and I genuinely believed that war would soon become a thing of the past.

Maybe there was too much ego and not enough heart, or too much money to be made for some by keeping war alive? Sadly, the Peace Movement that I expected would help transform the world I grew up in, all but disappeared, and what remained was another unrealised dream in my yellow brick road.

Through the seventies and eighties, I noticed the rise of meditation groups in the Western world. I spent about twelve years practicing Transcendental Meditation, believing that we would all be living in collective enlightenment in the foreseeable future.

Mainstream religion was definitely losing its appeal for some, and when the New Age Movement emerged, many—me included—abandoned religion and claimed to be 'spiritual' instead. We believed that being spiritual was less dogmatic than the control of religion that we had grown up with.

As the end of the nineties drew closer, an increasing number of us believed in 'The Shift'. However, it was business as usual, and once again disappointment arose as the new millennium arrived, and the Promised Land of a Peaceful Ascended Humanity, remained an elusive myth.

There are followers of religion who have truly found the LOVE of God in their hearts, and there are spiritual seekers who have found the Truth and surrendered to LOVE, but many of us still don't realise how strong fear is, and how much allegiance we still give to this god of deception and control who has wreaked havoc in our 3rd dimensional world of separation.

'Fear is: False Evidence Appearing Real,' a well-used quote for which I cannot find an original source. A Course in Miracles teaches there are only *two emotions, Love and fear*, (T-p.147) but only one of them is truly real. It also teaches: *'All healing is essentially the release from fear.'* (T-p.23)

Can we truly forgive ourselves for all the times we have ever chosen separation over Oneness, fear over Love, suffering over Joy? And if we do, will the weapons of war and hate in the world be finally surrendered, melt and dissolve? And if this happens, will Loving Peace and 'Brotherhood of Man' melt the remaining boundaries of separation between religions, states, and countries?

Surrendering the childhood conditioning that we are often unaware of is not an easy task, especially when we live in a world whose controllers depend on our disempowerment and obedience. So what is stopping us? Oh, yes … fear, that weapon of mass destruction, used as a weapon of mass distraction that has been keeping us in the matrix!!!

Let us remember that in every moment, we have a choice as to who to give our allegiance. Only then will we begin to remember our true purpose.

In *Snapshots* there are light hearted moments, deeply emotional moments, and some up front moments. I sincerely hope you enjoy the read.

POETRY

Ask me no Questions and I'll Tell you no Lies

The world is going crazy,
the Truth is well disguised!
If you ask me no questions,
I will tell you all no lies.

We're living in a nanny state;
Big Brother makes the rules,
and laughs demoniacally;
he treats us all like fools.

Manipulating media
is dazzling all the folk.
It shields us from a truth that
would make you want to choke!

Monsanto wants to rule the world
controlling all the food,
re-defining nature's job
with motives dark and crude!

Religions teach the love of god
and promise after-life
for those who kill with sword, and bomb,
and fall upon the knife.

Politicians play charades
and hope that we won't guess
what's really going on beneath
the global ruling mess!

Michael Moore succinctly shows
in *Fahrenheit 9/11*,
the war on terror gave us Fear,
The weapon of mass destruction.

NASA tries to hide the truth
of Mars and Moon and Space,
while men in black move stealthily
to reinforce their case.

Have you seen the chem trails
as they linger in the sky, while
the planes that may have dropped them
have long since flown by?

Do you know what's in the food
that comes packed and prepared?
You pick it from the supermarket
shelf when it's all dead.

What's happened to our Eden,
was it ever really here?
Now it's $war and $politics;
will $they ever care?

Ask yourselves the questions,
and then search out the Truth.
The world is going crazy,
do you want to follow suit?

My Red Gum Friend

Are you out there old friend?

You used to stand on the side of the road in Bullaburra
in your resplendent Angophoric beauty.

I used to drive along the highway into Bullaburra
and there you were. My heart would lift and my face
would smile every time I saw you waiting for me to pass by.

I still remember driving up the road from Lawson that day.
I came around the corner into Bullaburra, saw you
and cried. They told us you were going to be cut down for
the road widening. I was so sad and bereft … I wasn't
ready to lose you … I couldn't understand why they weren't
building the road around you!

'They're going to cut you down,' I sobbed
as my car got closer and closer.
'I know,' you replied. 'Don't worry, it's all ok.'
So I told myself to not worry.
It's in the bigger plan, and my friend is
moving on to another experience.

Where are you now, friend?

The highway extensions are finished
and the new pedestrian walkway to the station is complete.

If you were human, there would be a plaque
on the side of the road to remind us all that you had
once 'passed' through. I don't need a plaque.
You are still in my heart, and I am grateful for having known you.

Do you remember the day I came by with my camera?
I parked on the other side of the road and ran across
to say goodbye and to take some photos of you.

I marvelled at your natural beauty, at the artistic patterns
of your branches, at the strength of your presence.
Then I touched you gently and said 'I love you.'

I was visiting my friend on death row.

Soon they came and placed the ropes and chains
around you. Then one day, the sentence was delivered
and your mortal frame was cut down.

Bullaburra means 'clear day,'
and with the road widening, we have a clear way.
Life comes and goes, and we
all hope to make a difference along the way.

You have bought joy to the hearts of many a traveller as we
drove up and down the Blue Mountains, Bullaburra highway.
Thank you my beautiful red gum friend
for the difference you have made.

Do me no Favours

Welcome to the modern world;
but have things really changed?
Oh ancient days of life corrupt,
the song remains the same.

Politics and business, ah
it's such a rotten game.
Old Shakespeare spoke of Denmark,
but the rot remains the same.

It's spread throughout the Eastern world
and conquered in the West,
insidiously controlling
and dumbing down the beast

called hu man and wo man,
the breeders and the drones;
kept in jobs 'just over broke'
kept 'wanting' by the clones

who worship power and glory way
above this sacred earth.
Those heartless ones who rule the world
and reign with fear and dearth.

'All hail the god of money,
let's manipulate the weak.
Let's feed their insecurities
and in our grip do keep!

Let's trick them in believing that
they're worthless piles of shit.
Their heads will bow and they will spend
their money and their wit,

while we sit back and laugh and
jest and ridicule them all.
They know not what is happening;
they haven't since the fall.'

People, please, hear heaven's plea.
It's time that we awaken!
We've played the games of 'big' and 'small'
and all we've got is broken …

hearts and dreams we cannot reach
and fear that rules our actions.
It keeps us small and cowering,
lost in divided factions.

Let's forgive our broken hearts.
Let's stand tall, strong and free.
Lay down our swords of blame and guilt;
Know 'Peace begins with Me!'

We're equal in the eyes of LOVE
no better than, or worse.
It's time to trust that we deserve!
Let's drop that pointless curse, of

'Woe betide, he's better than me
I've got to see him fall.'
Don't sell your soul to the devil
making contracts with the pall!

Conglomerates and concrete malls
de-naturalise society.
They've veiled and raped our precious earth
and led to impropriety.

Stop looking for the answers
in the world of 'pomp' and 'man'.
Come rest inside your own true heart
and know and trust you can …

listen to that still small voice.
It calls to set you free.
Be still a while and know thy Self.
You are more than you believe!

Heaven waits for open hearts
to lovingly embrace
our world of change and judgment,
and heal the human race.

You're stronger than your fear dictates.
Don't give it any power,
for only then can heaven on earth
realise its final hour.

The heart of mother Gaia
will reach her heavenly realm,
and those of us here living,
will be lifted out of hell.

The time is now! Tarry not
for trumpets sound the call
to Grace and Joy and LOVE complete.
We do not need to fall.

The truest power is not of earth,
or fear, control, or greed.
The truest power is your own heart.
Know: Peace begins with Me.

Pull Your Finger Out!

Pull your finger out,
the earth is going down!
Our mother ship is listing
and twisting all around!

Those Agents of the hard of sight
with dollars in their eyes!
They're fracking us, can't you see,
and speeding our demise!

The men in black with their recruits
are walking hand in hand;
They're harvesting our mother's gas
and poisoning our land.

Remember Midas and his gold?
He loved it all too much.
His dream became a life of hell;
oh woe the Midas touch!

Contaminated water is
too hard to purify.
The damage to all living life,
too hard to qualify.

Pull your finger out,
the earth is going down!
Our mother ship is shaking
and falling underground!

'Oh my god, we've never had
such earthquakes here before.
Safe? Be dammed, they're fooling us!
They're rotten to their core!

Hydraulic fracturing, they say
is safe for land and sea.
They've tried to fool the people but
they won't be fooling me.

Don't you drink that water from
the nearby natural well,
and don't you feed your crops with
that toxic spew from hell!'

'It's safe,' they say. 'Our research
shows there is no ill effect.
Our scientists? We pay them well
to set your minds at rest.'

'So tell me why my family's sick,
our favourite cats have died?!
You think we're going to trust you now?
You really have a hide!'

Pull your finger out,
the earth is going down!
Our mother ship is trembling
and grieving for her crown.

O' water pure and healthy soil;
a fading memory.
Is it now a helpless plight,
a hopeless reverie?

But what's the sweet alternative?
Well, there's a sobering thought!
Tesla found free energy
which Morgan quickly 'bought'

then 'sold' us electricity
across the developing globe.
Another scheme of lies and chains
from underneath his robe!

What's happened to the Promised Land?
I can't help looking back!
Coal Seam Gas is just fool's gold;
I think we've all been fracked!

So pull your finger out,
the earth is going down!
Our mother ship is calling us,
we've got to gather round
and join in voice and harmony;
let's sing the freedom song.
Lift your hearts and feel the Truth
before we get it wrong!

Weeping Tigers

Machines are mastering
Fact is transforming
Fiction is emerging
Reality is changing

Racists are dividing
Religions are defiling
The truth is hiding
Hell is in the living

Men are killing
Children are dying
Cemeteries are crowding
Women are crying

Despair is defeating
Fear is isolating
Hopelessness is reigning
Suicide is separating

The media is deceiving
Politics is confusing
Big Business is controlling
The banks are governing

Vaccinations are infecting
GMO's are sterilising
Roundup is ruling
The bees are dying

The rivers are poisoned
Our soil is toxic
The mines are leaking
Our babies are allergic

The sea is emptying
The fish are drowning
The fishermen are leaving
The gluttons are eating

Whales are beaching
Birds are falling
Tigers are weeping
The alarms are sounding

Coal is tarring
Petrol is corrupting
NATO is hypnotising
Money is manipulating

Rainforests are shrinking
Our lungs are labouring
Fires are burning
The future is uncertain

The God of Love has been deposed
by the god of money where 'anything' goes

But the earth is shaking
Woman is awakening
Truth is emerging
Times they are a changing

Heaven is calling
The angels are helping
We are slowly listening
Heavy hearts are melting

Karma is dissolving
Forgiveness is releasing
Salvation is enveloping
Joy is fulfilling

The sun is always shining
God is always Loving
The Earth is always giving
LOVE is always healing

A Plea for Help

Whoever is out there coming from LOVE,
PLEASE help me. I've had enough
of fear, worry, and thinking life sucks.
I see no way out! I just wanna give up.

But I know deep down hiding in my gut
is the message of LOVE that's needing to come out
to remind me of the Truth that I Am good enough!
It's time to break free of this limiting stuff.

I fell to the ground in hopeless reverie.
I wanted to die so that I would be free
of the pain and suffering that I was making real,
thinking 'It's too hard for me to heal.'

But something started whispering in my ears.
A warm glowing feeling of LOVE dried my tears.
For a very brief moment I felt no fear,
and thought: 'Is God real? Does he really care?'

I don't know what to do to help me heal.
Please, PLEASE help me to know what's truly real.
I'm moving my body now so that I can kneel
and look up to Heaven and the Universal realm.

My arms are open wide as I'm looking above
the trials and tribulations that stopped me feeling Loved.
There's got to be an answer deep within my Soul.
Help me melt the armour that keeps me dark and cold.

Suicide is tempting, but what will it achieve?
The people who love me would drown in shock and grief.
It's time I need to learn how to LOVE Me!
God, PLEASE help me to heal and set me free.

Father my Father

You don't listen to me when I cry
'Big boys are brave!'
My heart is breaking and I cannot find the love to help me heal.

I see the Light of God in the beauty of a rose.
How can I be sure of what I know if I cannot speak?
'Flowers are for sissies!'

Why won't you hug me?
Tell me that you love me.
Not for what I do, but for who I am?

I want to play with the girls down the road.
I like their dolls.
Why do I get the feeling you don't approve?

I want you to play with ME.
We always have to play your games.
I don't always want to be just like you.

You make me scared when I don't do what you want.
You disappear in clouds of red and black.
I want the peace back.

Girls are allowed to hit me.
You tell me I cannot hit them back.
Why do I feel confused?

Sometime's your world is fun.
Sometimes it's harsh and cruel.
Sometimes I wonder how I'm going to survive.

It's not safe for me to feel.
I'm not accepted when I'm real.
I'll have to close the door.

Why do you like to drink?
What's that funny smell when Uncle Joseph smokes?
Why does my cousin sniff glue?

No-one here remembers where we've come from.
I feel so out of place.
I'll have to forget if I'm going to make it.

'Don't you tell me what to do!
Get your hands off me you …
I'm leaving this place!'

The Affluent Society

'I'm proud to be an Aussie!'
I often hear you say;
meat pies and barbeques
the order of the day!

But what about the rubbish
left laying all around;
paper bags and plastics
left blowing on the ground?

'We've got the greatest beaches!'
I often hear you boast.
You crowd them in the sunshine
and sail them in your boat.

But what about the plastics
left floating out to sea;
swallowed up by fish and bird
who see them as a feed?

'Gotta stand by your mates!'
I often hear you cry;
'I've got your back, you've got mine;
we gotta do or die!'

But what about the animals
left poisoned on the land?
Coal seam gas, chemicals
and mate-ship's sleight of hand?

'Holdens are our heroes!'
I've heard you shout for years.
Aussie born and Aussie bred,
It's brought you close to tears!

But what about the highways?
Now where's the Aussie pride?
Macca's packs, bottles smashed
and nappies on the side!

'We're bloody good at rugby'
I've heard you jump for joy.
'Aussie Aussie Aussie,
Oi Oi Oi!'

But are you good at cleaning
up the mess that's at your feet
as you stand to leave the sports ground
and spill into the street?

'Aussie folk are battlers'
I often hear you claim.
Chips are down, you rally round
and make it through the pain.

But what about the young ones
who are riding on the trains,
graffiti-ing the carriages
and scratching window panes?

You proudly wear the Aussie flag
and chant the Aussie pride.
Then go indoors into a house
that's nice and clean inside.

But parks and streets and beaches
lay burdened with your trash.
Your children learn to follow
with decisions blind and rash.

'Australia Day, we're the best;'
it comes round once a year.
What if it came every day,
would you learn to care?

Real pride is Self-respect
so take a second glance,
and be that mate to nature;
give us all a second chance.

Our true backyard is limitless;
our family ain't that small!
Our mate the earth is crying
out, can't you hear her call?

The Southern Cross reminds us
of our place under the sun.
The earth, the plants and animals;
we all live here as One!

So be proud of your Family,
your Country and your cars
and this Planet that we live on
underneath the Southern Stars!

Boys in Blue

Little boys in blue,
in your jelly bean cars.
For whom do you really work?
Who **do** you think you are?

I saw you in full force today,
waiting on the side.
The pollies coffers getting low?
They sent you out to hide?

Little boys in blue
with your jelly bean stars.
How many did you get today
by sitting in your cars

and watching your technology
in case a driver errs,
so you can get your quota
and fill the pollies purse?

Little boys in blue
with your jelly bean dreams.
What made you want to be a cop?
Is it what it seems?

Driving fast and catching hoons,
and carrying a gun.
Firing off the tasers
when a robber's on the run.

Little boys in blue
with your jelly bean books.
Trying hard to be good kids
and catching all the crooks.

Do you ever tell a lie?
Do you ever steal?
Do you ever speed while driving?
Bet you'll never tell.

Little boys in blue,
in your jelly bean cars.
For whom do you really work?
Who **do** you think you are?

The Beginning of the End

'Eat drink and be merry for tomorrow you may diet.'

Great! Bloody stupid fridge magnet! What was I thinking?
Yeah, ok … It was funny at the time, but that was last year.
Dieting was a joke. Crap! Now tomorrow is today.
D day … Diet day … Death day!

How long did I say I would do this for?
Why did I even agree to it in the first place?

Roseanne said she wants to lose weight so she can fit into her Wedding dress. This is ridiculous. Why didn't she just get a bigger size, one that really fitted her!

So, we were out having a drink, and I'm her best friend. She said, 'Wouldn't it be great if we both lost weight for my Wedding. The photos would look fantastic!'

I thought to myself, 'Shayne the best man is such a hottie.'

I thought so when I met him two years ago when he was going out with Alicia. Roseanne told me just before Christmas that they had broken up. I'm sure it's sad for one of them, but I didn't lose any sleep over it.

'Go on a diet 'cos I'm partnering Shayne at the wedding!'
That was logically strategic and seemed like a really fantastic idea at the time.

Groan! Diets … deprivation … disaster … depression.
This fast track diet is soooo limiting for me!

No more chocolate.
No more cheesecake.
Oh no! No more ANZAC biscuits, my life-saving pick me ups!

Oh my god, surely this is the beginning of the end!
… I think I'll start tomorrow!

The Pot of Gold

I AM the pot of Gold at the end of my rainbow
and my responsibility to myself is to KNOW THIS TRUTH
by discovering the wonderful treasures within.

Pain is the dragon that protects this gold from being discovered,
but this dragon is illusion and illusion recognised must disappear.
Yet this cannot happen if I try to fight and banish it because
that is separation and the very thing I fear the most.

LOVE is the transformative power in Creation and
Love is who I AM,
and it is in the light of Love and Acceptance
that I must face this dragon and no longer be afraid of it.

When I have shone the light of Love and Acceptance upon it
and embraced it in my heart, the dragon disappears
and what remains is Peace and Joy and the knowing that
I AM the pot of gold at the end of my rainbow,
and the dragon protecting it was me.

Step Up

Step up,
fall down,
on the wheel
go round and round.

Bright night,
dark day.
Will the pain
please go away!

Rain clouds,
rainbows.
Where is God?
Hell, no-one knows.

Hard fear,
soft trust.
Find the truth.
I know I must

breathe in
breathe out.
What's my name?
What's love about?

Looking here,
looking there,
cannot find it
anywhere.

Sit down,
give up.
What's the point?
I'm out of luck.

Let go,
big sigh,
body slump,
there's no more flight.

Be still.
Feel peace.
Smiling heart,
I feel release.

No pain,
no fight.
Just relaxed
and feeling light.

Joy moves,
feet dance.
Body whirls
in Love's entrance.

Sun shines,
face glows.
Where is God?
Well, now I know!

Soft night,
bright day.
All the pain
has gone away.

Step up,
step down.
LOVE's in charge,
I'm smiling now.

Still Dithering

Do I go or do I stay?
Will the time please go away!

Oh God my mind has gone a blank;
surely this is just a prank.

What's the time; where do I go?
Heaven help me, I don't know

quite what to do in times like these.
Guess I'd better find my keys.

Or should I walk and catch the bus?
That would surely stop the fuss

of circling round in the dark
and hoping hard to find a park.

Oh woe is me in winter's grip.
This outing's giving me the pip.

Sinking sun and warm embrace
of gas flames dancing on my face;

Comfy chair and TV guide;
would I rather stay and hide?

Dear me the time is whizzing by;
the bus will leave me; gotta fly.

Ah, there's the invite on my wall.
What? Oh stupidest one of all.

Today is not the date I see.
Bloody hell, oh silly me!

Next week is when the dance is on.
Phew, how did I get that wrong?

Cup of tea… now let me think
as I'm walking to the sink.

This whole affair has been hard work!
Am I really trying to shirk?

Maybe I don't want to go!
I'll email now and tell him 'no'.

No more dithering for me.
What a sigh of big relief!

I Wouldn't Be a Woman for Quids

I wouldn't be a woman for quids,
but then every man has his price.
Maybe for just a day or two
it could really be very nice

to wear those long sexy dresses
and play with my face all day,
making sure of no mascara messes
by wiping those tears clean away.

I'd put on my shoes and go running
up and down central park,
getting used to my new anatomy,
though I'd never go in after dark!

Might have to squeeze into stilettos,
or wear skimpy togs at the beach.
The men would all give me the eyeball;
how do I stay out of reach?

I'd have to try not to get pregnant.
Imagine the pain and the weight?
It's bad enough giving birth early;
what if the baby comes late?

But then I'd be feeling pre-menstrual
with out-of-control swings of mood.
Men can be harsh and unfeeling,
and really, very terribly rude.

I'd start to feel like a leper
and fixate on my wrinkles and bum.
No, I wouldn't want to be a woman,
… that could be really quite dumb!

I wouldn't be a woman for quids,
but then every man has his price.
Maybe for just a moment or two
it might really be very nice?

A Memory (4a Wilkinson Street)

The lonely cry of a seagull
as it wings its way overhead
striking a respondent chord in my memory

of summer days in Oriental Bay
when life, though often painful,
was young and uncomplicated.

Strolling under infinite blue,
an endless sun penetrating life itself
with its all-embracing warmth and permeating light.

A lazy harbour sea meditating in the harmony;
stiller than a sheet of glass
yet bursting with potential fluidity

and I, drinking of this splendour
through every cell
through every fibre
deep into my very soul.

Ah, the sweet taste of nostalgia.

When I Stopped Running

When I stopped running
I fell to the ground,
and curling into a foetal position
I held my knees, and rocked, and sobbed.

I sobbed for all the times I felt alone.
I sobbed for all the times I felt unworthy.
I sobbed for all the times I felt unloved.
I sobbed for all the times I felt God had abandoned me.

When I stopped running
I noticed my heart,
and terrified that it was going to break,
I held my chest, and sat, and cried.

I cried for all the times I felt let down.
I cried for all the times I felt passed by.
I cried for all the times I felt forgotten.
I cried for all the times I felt I had let myself down.

When I stopped running
I saw the flowers,
and shocked at the beauty and grace I'd been missing,
I lay down, closed my eyes, and sighed.

I sighed for all the times I ran away.
I sighed for all the times I blamed myself.
I sighed for all the times I got it wrong.
I sighed for all the times I forgot that I AM Love.

When I stopped running
I felt the peace
and drinking in the warmth from a bright golden sun,
I felt my heart, stood tall, and gave thanks.

I gave thanks for the friends who stand by me.
I gave thanks for the family who love me.
I gave thanks for the joy that surrounds me.
I gave thanks for the love that is healing my broken heart.

When I stopped running
I felt the bliss
and melting into pure, transcendent LOVE,
I surrendered, knew God, and laughed.

I laughed because now I AM joy.
I laughed because now I AM peace.
I laughed because now I AM love,
I laughed because now I AM free.

When I stopped running, my life began!

My Christmas Wish

'The sun has slowly risen
in the heart of humanity.
Trust is now a given
and Joy is the currency.

The walls have broken down
to reveal collective memory,
that LOVE is the one true way
to Heavenly Divinity.

Arms of hate and war have
been thrown down indefinitely
while enemies and foes have
embraced each other gratefully.

The strength of the kingdom
is within us individually;
our joined hands and open hearts
are sharing it collectively.

Forgiveness led the way
and Acceptance unconditionally
brings to life on planet earth
a Joy that is so heavenly.

The Song of Peace can now be heard;
it is the greatest symphony.
It hums from deep within the earth
and radiates entirely

through every plant and every rock
and every tree, and finally,
through every bird and animal
and every human family.

*Intuition guides us through the
cycles of adversity.
Human beings now wisely live
the sage prayer of Serenity.*

*Laughter reigns and Wisdom leads
with Gratitude and Purity.
Man, nature, bird and beast
live in Greater Harmony!'*

I live in hope that one day soon
my Christmas Wish, still fantasy,
will manifest as Heaven on Earth
and become my True Reality.

Ascension

Like-minded people with a
Heart and Soul connection
Here to help humanity
Reach the 5th dimension

As we walk through the corridor
Of the 4th dimension
Healing wounds and trauma
From our ego's separation

In 3d 'reality' that's
Really an illusion
A hologram that's ruled by fear
Chaos and confusion

We came to heal our family lines
Ancestral pain and trauma
Plus remaining timeline blocks from
Negative past life karma

Forgiveness paves the way from
Insanity to Sanity
Holding on to angry rage
Will pause the 5d Journey

Forgiving others for what they did
That 'caused' our pain and trauma
Helps us move along the path
And frees us to remember

That we're the one who made it real
And added to the karma
If we want to change the world
We have to live our Dharma

Self-forgiveness heals us
And puts us back on track
Self-Love and Acceptance
Dissolves our fear of lack

The God of LOVE is WHO WE ARE
We just need to remember
And BE and SEE that Truth
As our Daily Living Mantra.

SHORT STORIES

I Was There!

I'm a woman on my own and … well … there are some things you get really tired of doing.

I mean … I could have asked a male friend … I do have one or two who are single. God knows I've certainly done it myself several times…What else do you do when there's no one else to help you out? But you know… I decided to treat myself. I'd never done this sort of thing before, and I would never have thought about it. But, there I was driving past one day and I saw the sign. 'Oh my God,' I thought. 'Could I really do THAT?'

Then I got too busy and … well … I don't go down to that part of town very often. And besides, I'm not used to paying for it. In fact, I've never had to pay for it before. But it started playing on my mind. You know how it goes; something you decide you want to do, but don't have quite the gumption to allow yourself to do it, so backwards and forwards it rolls in your mind. Well, today was the day that it stopped rolling! I was going to be driving down to the city and would be travelling past THAT part of town … if I turned first right instead of second right!

My mind was definitely made up. I was determined to go straight to the establishment when I arrived in the city.

The sun was shining as I drove down the hill. The traffic flow was even and moving at a respectable pace, not like the congestion you get in rush hour, thank goodness … I left it till late morning just to be on the safe side.

I turned right down THE road and then left at the lights, thinking that I would be able to drive in the back way. 'Wrong! One way street on this side,' so I had to drive round the block in order to come in on the opposite side of the road. (No, this is not a sign … keep going!)

I arrived at the establishment and found a place to park my car. I walked up to the reception desk and a gentleman came to greet me. He had such sparkling blue eyes and a warm, ruddy complexion…in a glowingly healthy way. I can tell you, it was such a relief to find someone more my age. The young ones just don't seem to understand the same.

He put me at ease right away. He was confident and self-assured, and seemed to really like his work. I could tell that he was experienced. He listened to my story, and after hearing what I wanted, he thoughtfully told me how much it would be, and how I might as well have these other extras as they came with this particular package.

Why not, I thought. As he said, I was paying for it anyway, so I might as well get my money's worth!

He very assuredly told me it would take one hour, and I followed him to the counter … to get the financials out of the way.

An hour later I returned to the front desk, and THERE WAS MY CAR, all shiny and sparkling. I had forgotten how deeply blue the car really was because it had been many months since I had given it a good wash. I had definitely become used to seeing the streaks of dirt and the layers of dust, and the consequential loss of depth of the real and vibrant colour of the paintwork, which simply shone with the wonderful wax job he'd given it.

He had done such a good job on the inside windows as well as the outside. I was willing to do the vacuuming, but as he had explained to me, if I wanted the inside windows done, for the price I was going to be charged, I might as well have the inside detailed. How right he was!

It was so good to get back into the driver's seat and look around at the clean interior. He had done a better job of vacuuming, and a much better job of dusting than the intermittent whisk over I was giving my car of late. I'm so glad that I was brave enough and decided to pay for my car to be cleaned. Something tells me that I will be stopping off at that part of town a lot more often from now on!!

Lily the Barmaid

It was quarter past five on a Wednesday afternoon. The men who worked at the local factory had just knocked off for another day and several of them were piling into the Rose & Crown. Lily the barmaid greeted them one by one, and welcomed them in like they were her own family coming home after a hard day's work.

Lily had lived and worked at the pub for twenty-five years and knew each of the men by name. She was a buxom woman with generous hips. She usually wore her long brown hair tied up in a bun that sat on top of her head. Greying curls framed her open face, and offset the warm twinkle in her eyes.

Tom was the first in the queue of thirsty men reluctant to go straight home to their wives and families, or of those who didn't have anyone to go home to.

'Watcha having, Tom?' asked Lily.

'The usual thanks, Lily,' replied Tom, as he put his money on the bar.

He knew how much his drink cost and always tried to have the right amount of change to give to Lily.

As he picked up his pint of ale, he winked at her, and walked away to sit at a nearby table to relax.

'You're alright, Tom,' said Lily as he turned away.

She looked at Sam and Ian who were next in the queue.

'The same for us thanks, Lily,' they chorused. 'And a couple of bags of crisps,' added Ian.

Sam and Ian were the youngest of the lads who worked at the factory and were still in their apprenticeships. The older blokes gave them a bit of a tease at times, but they enjoyed having the youngins around. Surviving twins weren't very common in this town, and Sam and Ian were regarded somewhat as celebrities, not that they saw themselves like that!

Their Da used to work at the factory. 'That's why the foreman took you on,' their mother would say when she was chiding them for being late of a morning.

She missed her husband terribly some days. Dave was the love of her life. When they met, Emily couldn't believe that God could be so good to her. When Dave died that autumn day, she couldn't understand how God could be so cruel. Surely heart attacks only happened to older people?

Dave had loved Emily from the moment he first laid eyes on her. It was at the county fair, and she was pouring freshly squeezed orange juice into cups for sale. He thought his life couldn't get any better when she said 'Yes, I'll marry you!' and hugged him so tightly around his neck he thought he was going to choke. Well, that was his story anyway, and he recounted it often throughout their marriage, looking at her with a warm smile and tender eyes as he spoke. That was before he saw his newborn twins for the very first time.

Men can be standoffish with their affections, especially when it comes to male children. But Dave was never afraid to show how grateful he was to have his boys and how much they meant to him.

Dave and Emily tried to have more children, but somehow she was never able to carry another baby to full term. It was a sad time back then. One day he said to her, 'I don't know what God's plan is here, blossom. It's not your fault, so no point in feeling bad. Let's be grateful for what we have,' and he always was.

Lily placed the two pints of ale on the bar with the crisps. 'Thanks lads,' she smiled and handed Sam his change.

'Thanks, Lily,' they chorused and moved off to sit with Tom, each carrying a pint of ale and a bag of crisps.

The factory was an important business in their small town. It provided work for a lot of the men and kept other businesses afloat, especially the local pub! As long as there were men to work there, the factory would continue to keep the town alive.

By now the queue had all but gone, and the pub was alive with laughter and the screams of admonishment and disbelief as darts hit the board and missed the bulls-eye.

Lily enjoyed these Wednesday evenings at the pub. Wednesday was mid-week. 'Gotta celebrate being closer to the end of the week than at the beginning,' the men would often say if they went up to the bar for a refill before going home.

Suddenly it was the last man standing. 'Last but not least, aye Jack. Watcha having, love?' said Lily.

'Give us a pint and a bag of peanuts, my beauty,' replied Jack, and placed his money on the bar.

Lily knew all their stories. Jack, for instance, was unhappily married to Edna. They had to get married. It was their final year of school and they had left the school dance together, early. Edna's father blamed Jack and told him they would be getting married before the end of spring and that he had better take good care of her, or else!

Jack did his best, or so he thought. But once the baby was born, he found it difficult to find his place. Then suddenly, the years had gone by. The oldest was now living abroad and there were three kids left at home. Edna was always a good and capable mother. Jack felt that he did his job by going to work and keeping them with food on the table and a roof over their heads. He was grateful for the pub and being able to hang out with some of his mates from work. This is where he felt most comfortable.

Tom walked up to the bar with his empty glass. 'That was quick, Tommy m'boy,' said Jack as he picked up his Guinness and peanuts.

'Gotta be in to win, and I beat youse all tonight,' replied Tom as Jack moved off to find an empty seat.

Tom lived at home with his youngest daughter, Millie. His wife of twenty-three years had decided it was time for a change and went off with the librarian. That was two and a half years ago now. It was all very shocking really. He hadn't known any lesbians personally before, and didn't know he was married to one ... until she left.

'You should have had some idea, Tom,' said his friends. But he didn't. 'How do you know these things?' he would reply, but no one really knew the answer.

'Just give us half a pint thanks, Lily,' he said.

'Anything for you, Tom,' replied Lily with her warm demeanour and twinkling eyes.

It was twenty five years ago now since Lily moved into the town. She'd seen the ad for a live in barmaid in the local paper when she was on her way back from up north. She had stopped off to have lunch and give herself a rest. As she sat at the table, she picked up a copy of the local paper and started to read it. That's when she saw the ad flashing at her like a neon sign. She finished her cup of tea, went straight round to the pub and said, 'I want your job and I can start next week!'

Lily had been engaged to her childhood sweetheart. They used to be inseparable. Then Christian got himself a new job, one that took him down to the city once or twice a week. Lily noticed that Christian was becoming more and more preoccupied. She figured it was because of the responsibility of his job. Then three months before their wedding, he broke it off and moved in with a girl from the city. Lily was devastated. She hadn't seen it coming, and didn't know what to do.

She had no holidays left at work so she took leave without pay, and went up north to stay with an old family friend who lived on a country farm. This proved to be a very healing time for her, and by the time she drove away on her journey home, she felt stronger and able to face the world again.

As Lily was pouring Tom's half pint of ale, one of the other men arrived back at the bar.

'Move over Tom,' joked Bob. 'You're hogging up the bar, and the staff! Leave some room for me why don't ya?'

'In your dreams, Bob,' laughed Tom, pretending to block the way and force Bob back.

'Now boys, playtime's over,' smiled Lily as she put Tom's ale on the bar. 'Another pint for you Bob?' she asked.

Yep, filler up again,' said Bob. 'Gotta celebrate being closer to the end of the week than at the beginning!'

Tom waited until Bob left the bar. Looking around the room he noticed that the others were busy chatting and nursing their near-empty pints. He turned back to the bar, and looking Lily in the eye, he said, 'Do you ever get lonely, Lily?'

'Not with you lot around keeping me busy,' she joked. Tom didn't move.

'Yeah, I know what you mean, Tom,' she replied, meeting his gaze.

Lily liked Tom, a lot. She had for a long time, but he was married. Besides, it was safer for her to like someone unavailable; he couldn't up and leave her for another woman. He was never hers to begin with.

Tom continued. 'You're a fine woman, Lily. What would you say if I asked you to marry me?'

Lily was taken quite by surprise at hearing this from Tom. There was no denying the increase in her heartbeat, and she hoped he wouldn't notice the flush that was uncontrollably beginning to colour her cheeks.

'Why, Tom, you sure know how to get a girl off guard,' she said turning her head and looking away.

'That's no answer!' said Tom intently.

Lily looked back at Tom and said, 'Well, Tom Williams, I might just say yes.'

Tom scrambled for something to reply with. He certainly hadn't thought this far when he decided he was going to ask Lily this question.

'Well then. I guess we better have lunch on your day off and get better acquainted,' he said with a pleasantly surprised feeling welling up in his chest.

'It's a date,' said Lily. 'You know where I live.'

Tom smiled. 'I'll pick you up at 11.30 a.m. and take you on a mystery tour.'

Feeling rather chuffed, Tom turned around and walked away from the bar, just as Jeff wandered up with his empty glass.

'Fine day today isn't it, Jeff,' said Tom as he passed by. Jeff looked at Tom with a quizzical look and watched him walk back to his table. Then he shrugged his shoulders, turned back, and walked up to the bar.

'Give us a refill thanks, young lady,' he flirted.

'You need to get your eyes tested,' laughed Lily, as she picked up Jeff's empty glass and filled it with ale.

Sitting on the Esky

Jill settled into her chair, and getting comfortable, she leaned back, and smiled at her two friends as they stood in front of the audience. With their guitars in hand, they introduced themselves and the first song in their ten minute set.

It had been a gloriously warm and sunny spring day. Winter was long and cold this year, and the promise of summer had seemed like such a torturous tease, but today had been magic; everyone was feeling it, and as Jill walked round the community market earlier that day, she saw the memory of summer was fresh and alive on the faces of everyone she passed.

After the market closed, the local Folk Club gathered where both local and visiting artists came to sing. Jill loved music and enjoyed this community gathering. She felt a sense of belonging at these events where people came together in their shared love for live music and performance.

The first number finished, and the audience clapped enthusiastically. Then the haunting melody of 'Somewhere over the Rainbow' began to float around the room, touching the hearts and memories of many of the people listening. Her friend's clear and dulcet tones carried Jill on a puffy white cloud across a sunny blue sky, back to the days when she was a young girl who dreamed dreams and imagined a life to come.

Like many girls of her generation, the rainbow had been a symbol of real hope and promise to Jill. She had grown up with this song, and used to imagine being discovered by Prince Charming. He would come and find her and sweep her away. They would have three, maybe four children—she didn't mind which—and they would live happily ever after.

The song played on and her memories returned her to the much-loved family outings at the beach in summer. She would sit on the esky looking out to sea, dreaming that she was on a boat and travelling to rendezvous with her betrothed. She had such faith in the power of her dreams back then. Life was supposed to be magic, and her trusting childhood innocence and well developed imagination, would not deter her from believing otherwise. How could she have known the turbulent waters that lay ahead of her?

As an adult, she had travelled to far off lands and believed it was Prince Charming that asked her to marry him. Alas, the dark cloud came when the charm eventually wore off and he sailed on to another port, alone.

There had been two subsequent suitors she felt sure were her Prince, but her experience was to prove her wrong. None of this made sense to Jill, and with an increasingly disillusioned and heavy heart, her childhood wonder and innocent hope had begun to erode.

The last line in the song echoed around the room. As she heard the words, Jill felt like she had been hit by a lightning bolt. She suddenly realised just how deeply she had come to believe that her dreams never came true. It shook her to her core. If she no longer believed in her dreams and her ability to have what she truly wanted, isn't that exactly what she was going to continue to create in her life? In that moment, she decided it was time to completely let go of the disappointments of her adult past.

Jill thought to herself "I **can** have what I want and my dreams **have** come true!"

As the audience clapped, Jill could feel a cellular change in her body. These new beliefs were taking hold and changing her future at warp speed. Feeling the promise of a new possibility, she joined in the applause, and smiled at her friends as they walked off the stage.

Breathing a warm and peaceful sigh, Jill decided to go for a walk to integrate what had just happened. There was a lot of nature around the suburb in which she lived, and now would be a great time to be walking in it. She waved to her friends and turned to leave the hall.

As Jill stood on the outside step, she saw a man walking towards her. He gazed briefly at her with warm, smiling eyes that stared directly into a part of her soul, a part that had been closed for what seemed like an eternity. She stepped aside as he walked past her and entered the room, then she continued walking towards the courtyard.

After a few steps, something told her to turn around. As she looked back into the room, Jill saw the man looking at her and their eyes met once again. They smiled at each other, and for a moment, everything around them seemed to disappear. A deep and knowing peace arose from within Jill's heart. Deciding to listen, she chose to trust once again, and walked back into the hall to meet her destiny.

There is Something I Must Tell You

As Ben got down on his knees and gently took her hands into his, Antoinette's heart sank. The eyes on her crestfallen face looked lovingly at this man who was asking her to marry him. She cast her mind back nine years, and realised that her worst nightmare had finally arrived!

After what seemed like an eternity to her, she replied, 'I have longed for this moment since the day we first met, and I have dreaded this moment since that day we first met. Before I reply, there is something that I must tell you.'

Antoinette withdrew her hands from Ben's eager hold, and turned away from the quizzical look that was forming on his face. She walked for a short distance and looked out at the ocean.

'You see Ben, God has played a cruel joke on me. I cannot have children!'

Ben looked perplexed as he tried to make sense of Antoinette's words. 'How do you know this?' he queried.

Antoinette turned back to face Ben, and with a sense of defeat about her countenance, she walked over to him and sat down.

'As you know, I was eight years old when my family moved to Australia. I missed France, and when I was eighteen, Sharon and I went on our European trip before we started University. We travelled to France, Greece, Italy, and back through England. It was such a fantastic time.

I took her to visit my home town, and we saw all the sites in Paris. We visited Notre-Dame Cathedral, and the Louvre, and Sharon loved the view from the Eiffel Tower. We were going to be studying Ancient History at Uni, so we searched through some of the ruins in Greece and Italy, and then we travelled to some ancient sites in England.'

Antoinette felt like she was on trial and wished she was confessing to the priest, not to the man she loved! At least the priest wouldn't be judging her, which is more than she could say for herself right now!

'I've never held my liquor well, which is why I don't drink it. At eighteen I was young and inexperienced. You see, we went to a club when we were in Italy. Sharon and I met two boys, and we spent the evening dancing and drinking. They drove us back to the hotel where we were staying. Sharon and the boy she was with, got out of the car and went into the hotel.

The car was parked in the hotel car park, and the boy I was with started to kiss me. I kissed him back, and he started to … anyway. In my drunken state, I had sex for the first time, with a boy I hardly knew, in a country that was foreign to me.

Ben's face looked like he'd seen a ghost and he moved backward to create a little distance between him and Antoinette.

'Three months later,' she continued, 'I found out I was pregnant. I couldn't believe it. What was I going to do? Uni had just started, and as Sharon pointed out, my whole life was ahead of me. I couldn't tell my parents, they would have been mortified, especially after funding my trip! We heard of a doctor in private practice that did abortions, and Sharon came with me. Oh my god, it was awful. My parents thought I was staying at Sharon's for a few days. There were complications and it left me damaged and unable to have children.' Antoinette began to sob.

Ben stiffened and stood up. 'What do you mean God played a cruel joke on you? It sounds like you did that to yourself. I can't believe what I am hearing, you can rot in hell!' Ben put the engagement ring back into his pocket and stormed off.

'Cut,' said the Director. 'That was Great guys. Xavier, now that I've seen the break up, I wonder how much more effective it might be if you throw the ring away instead of putting it in your pocket. I know we've been following the script, but tossing the ring might just make it more dramatic, and final.'

'OK, boss,' replied Xavier.

'Take it from: "What do you mean God played a cruel joke on you?"' said the director.

'And here, throw this pebble instead of the ring until we're ready for the final take.'

Checkmate

It was Sunday morning and Michael lay propped up in his hospital bed. The crisp white top sheet lay slightly dishevelled over his tired body. An oxygen tank stood beside his bed; he held tightly to a mask and breathed as if his life depended on it.

He found himself remembering the first time he ever smoked a cigarette. God, he felt so grown up, just like his dad. It was summer holidays, and he and his friend Johnny, were down the beach with a couple of smokes they he had sneaked out of his father's packet. Fifteen years old and knew it all, but really knew nothing of any real consequence.

They were all staying at his grandmother's place at the beach. He and Johnny had managed to find a moment when no one was in the lounge, just a packet of his father's smokes. Johnny kept a look out while Michael opened the packet and quickly pulled out two crisp white cigarettes. He immediately put them in his pocket where the packet of matches that he had 'procured' earlier from his grandmother's pantry, were waiting excitedly. 'Johnny and I are off to the beach. See you when we get back,' he called out.

As they walked down the road to where the sand met the tar-sealed cul-de-sac, Michael could hear his heart beating. He wasn't used to doing things like this. His father could be a hard bastard at times, and Michael was terrified of getting him so riled up that the fists would come out and backhand him. He tried not to think of this as they walked quickly down the sand dunes and off to the tree at the end of the beach.

No-one could see them here as they climbed the tree and sat in its branches, feeling as if they had gone to another planet.

'How's it going in there, mate?'

Michael looked over to his friend Johnny and breathed heavily. 'I was remembering the very first time you and I ever had a smoke. Do you remember? We were staying at Grammy's beach house and you and I snuck off to the tree with a couple of dad's fags.'

'Yep, I sure do,' replied Johnny. 'How grown up did we think we were, eh?'

'You were more grown up than me, mate,' said Michael through laboured breathing. 'You quit the next year, you smart bugger.'

'Yeah, well it never really grabbed me did it? I preferred the stuff in those little brown bottles as it turned out, until Julie came along.

Michael thought about Julie and Johnny. She was a lucky girl. In fact, all four of the kids were lucky too. Johnny was such a good father. Michael thought about his own two kids and the two failed marriages that produced them, and wondered how different things might have been if he had have moved out of his father's shadow years ago.

'What did I do to deserve this, eh mate?'

'We've tried to have this conversation before haven't we, Micko.' Johnny looked at his friend with compassion in his eyes. He knew the struggles Michael had experienced in his life. He'd had a few of his own throughout his sixty-six years, but somehow, he managed to get on top of things. Michael had seemed to hold something back all these years which denied him a true freedom and relaxation in life.

At sixty-five, he should have been looking forward to enjoying his retirement and the new relationship with his grandchildren, not staring at the lid of his coffin. At least one good thing had come out of the emphysema, he thought. Michael and his son Tony had been distant for many years, but since Michael had started to become ill, the two men had become much closer.

Johnny remembered how grateful he was that it was not his own father who was killed on the motorway that night, and how numb and disbelieving Michael was when his mother told him the news. Life for Michael with his father, wasn't easy. He could be a nasty cuss, that's for sure. But, a father is a father nevertheless, and when the bastards go and die on you before your twenty first birthday, it's a bit of a shock to the system.

'I'm going to ask you that question again, Micko,' said Johnny. 'Your father has been lurking in the shadows most of your life. Even before he died you were a bit of a train wreck at times.' Michael looked at his friend and started to feel tears welling up in his eyes. 'What do you regret the most about your father?' asked Johnny.

Michael held tightly to the mask on his face and breathed hard to get some oxygen. There was no strength left to deny the tears and they started to roll down his cheeks. He began to sob quietly and as deeply as his failing breath would allow. Johnny quietly grabbed some tissues from the cabinet that stood at the side of the hospital bed and gently wiped his friend's eyes and cheeks. After a few minutes the sobbing abated and Michael spoke. 'I never had the chance to tell him that I loved him.'

Johnny looked at his friend, feeling like a priest that had just heard someone's very first confession. 'Well done, mate,' he said. There was tenderness in his voice as he continued. 'You've carried that little secret for forty five years, and it was too fucking heavy to fit in that coffin with you.'

Michael reflected over his life, and realised with gratitude what a gift Johnny had been to him. They had met at school when they were eleven years old and been best friends ever since. Sure they had had some different experiences as they had gotten older, but Johnny was always there for him. And hadn't they had some fun!!!

Michael stretched out his right hand towards Johnny and said, 'Thanks mate. You've been there for me most of my life. I wouldn't want to have done it without you.' Johnny took his hand and leaned over the bed, giving his friend a hug. He suddenly felt an emptiness at the thought of Michael not being there anymore, and noticed a sting in his own eyes.

He sat back on his chair beside Michael's bed, and held onto his hand. Michael looked across at the love in Johnny's eyes and realised that he truly loved this childhood friend who he had grown up with. 'Not a gay love! Christ, we were never THAT close,' he thought. But there was a new awareness here and he suddenly understood that love comes in many forms, and the loyalty and commitment he shared with Johnny, was deeper and more real than he had ever been aware of.

He took another deep breath of oxygen, and sighed. How appreciative he felt that Johnny was with him. 'I think this is checkmate,' said Michael. He squeezed his friend's hand lightly and looked at his warm blue eyes. He then closed his own, and exhaled for the very last time.

Johnny sat there staring at the peaceful look on Michael's face. He gently placed his friend's hand back on his body, and said, 'See you on the other side, mate. It'll be a while yet, but we'll have one hell of a party, eh.'

Stage Interlude

Romeo, O Romeo; where have you gone, my Romeo?

'Cut … You seem to have forgotten. Pine for Romeo and you give your power away. Can you feel the distortion in your energy?'

Bugger, of course. I should know better. After all, I was the Queen of co-dependence. Sigh. That feast of fairy stories I voraciously devoured as a child, and believed! It gave me nothing but heartache and indigestion as an adult. How was Prince Charming going to be able to find Sleeping Beauty if she was hiding in the ivory tower with Rapunzel, not feeling worthy of him loving her?

What people will do to not feel their true Self! Well, I've had my midlife crisis. I know about Prince Charming; he turned out to be a myth and the carriage was always a pumpkin. So, what in heaven was I thinking just a minute ago?

I've been waiting for King Charming to turn up. Ha! Isn't that just another delusional distraction? 'But King Charming is a man, not a boyish Prince that you can't trust,' was my excuse.

Mmmm. How can I truly expect a man to love me if I don't fully love and accept myself? Isn't that just another ticking time bomb waiting patiently to surprise me when I'm off in the fantasy (that I'm in denial of having, of course, and believing is real), and when I'm least expecting another wake up call, 'Surprise!' Geez I'm good!

I remember when Sleeping Beauty first began to wake up. What was it I wrote?

FIRST STEP

I have searched so long
for a glimpse of your face.

Each new morning I think
'Maybe today,'
but night comes—
the pillow catches my tears like blotting paper

and again I feel the familiar ache of loneliness
deep to the core of my Being
and suffer my pain alone
under the empty blanket of darkness.

In my dreams you sweep along and find me
and away we ride on your white stallion.

The Prince with his Sleeping Beauty,
Robin Hood rescuing Maid Marion.

A damsel in distress,
that's me.
Wanting to be saved from my loneliness and pain,
Told that I am loved,
shown I am worthy.

Discovered like Cinderella,
transformed like the Beast …

I asked to see your face last night.
To look upon your features,
and know the one who will bring meaning to my life
and make me whole,

and as you turned around,
the face I saw was my own.

Christ! That was over twenty years ago and I'm still getting wet when I go swimming; that trickster ego!

'Don't be so hard on yourself? How long do you think it takes to be free of the patterns of childhood, of lifetimes, of generations, of tribal and cultural programming?'

Sigh. Yep, OK. Thanks. 'I'm sorry, I forgive me, I love me, I bless me.' Goodness, where would I be without forgiveness? No, don't remind me! Yes, do remind me. It's just so easy to forget that I AM LOVE already, and not that lonely little girl who had forgotten who she really was; who thought she was abandoned and unloved, and a shameful blight on creation.

The subconscious is a powerful distraction that tries to steer the game of life at every opportunity. Just like a game of snakes and ladders. You're on the home straight; you see 100 ahead of you and you're pumping. Liberation is at hand. 'I'm winning.' Then it's your turn. You throw the dice, and before you know it, you've landed on the head of the bloody snake and suddenly you're falling back into the middle of the game.

Well, I'm discovering that whinging and blaming don't help. Crucifixion, or freedom? I know which one calls me on to the end game. I just need to have a bit more quiet time so I can hear the reminder, 'Choose Love and Forgive.' That negative self talk can sure be loud and distracting!

I am LOVE, loveable, loving, and loved. Sigh. How on earth is it that I forget this?

'It's already in your heart. LOVE has its own sound, but you can't hear it with your ears. You can only feel it with an open and trusting heart.'

Yes, but …

'There are no buts. There are only two masters to follow—fear or LOVE—and only one of them is real; you know that. Follow the false idol and you're kept in a nightmare of separation and joylessness. The other brings you back to your true nature, PERFECT LOVE.

KNOW that you are intrinsically worthy. TRUST that LOVE holds you forever in its heart. ACCEPT that your TRUE SELF is always with you, and your small self is always safe. Any desire to believe otherwise is simply a 'miss take' in your divine allegiance.

There is no need to fear LOVE, LOVE does not judge; you do that very well. Remember, it's the non-trusting heart that worships fear, who places its seeker on the cross.'

Yes, you're right. I do know that. 'Nothing real can be threatened. Nothing unreal exists. Herein lies the peace of God,' and forgive myself whenever I notice I have inadvertently switched allegiance.

Thanks! I think it's time I put *The Life of Brian* back in the DVD player and remind myself to keep looking at that brighter side of life.

Turning Loneliness into Solitude

Seeing a newborn baby is one of the most innocent and precious moments we can experience in our lives. Feelings of purity and unconditional love are spontaneously evoked, as if a before-undiscovered tap in our hearts is instantly turned on, and an outpouring of love and nurturing is released.

This gift of new life with its pure trust and vulnerability, may remind the weary adult of the innocence that all life begins from. It may also raise the question: 'How on earth did I get here from there?'

A child is born with pure potential. Like a sculptor's clay, it is fashioned over time by the influences in its formative years. These include the joys of the parents' own magical child ... and the pains from their wounded inner child.

Then there are siblings, friends, social and tribal indoctrination, TV, advertising, and eventually, school!

Epigenetics tells us that a baby is already born with information coded in its genes and DNA. The choices it will make as a result of its upbringing and experiences in life, is what will determine which 'programs' it downloads and creates a life from.

The 'wounded child' is a human phenomenon. Something has happened in life that he has perceived, and translated, in a self-deprecating manner. In an instant, he has questioned his self–worth! Instead of shrugging off impossible untruths and remembering his intrinsic innocence with a pure and joyous laugh, he decides to believe he is unworthy, unlovable, not good enough, abandoned and damned forever.

Such beliefs become re-iterated. This new programme now unconsciously plays in his head like a CD stuck on repeat. His worldview grows from this distorted belief in his self-worth, and with the continuing input that he perceives from his environment, he helps to fashion the clay that he believes he is, and takes shape as he joins the world of his co-creation.

These self-deprecating, negative beliefs drive wounded children throughout their lives. Some strive to be bigger, better, successful, powerful. They are not afraid to be seen and heard, and seek to prove to themselves, via the world around them, that they are **not** the object of their judgement.

Other wounded children turn inward. They try to be invisible; try to hide their insecurity and loneliness behind such masks as the 'martyr' or the 'pleaser' in order to feel worthy and loveable. They may use the mask of the 'victim', choosing depression or addiction to numb the pain that arises from the belief in their intrinsic unworthiness, and the helplessness and hopelessness that arises as a result.

However a wounded child chooses to act in life, he is always operating from a perceived sense of lack and abandonment. Consequently, he will seek outside of himself in the attempt to fill the cup within his heart that he believes is empty.

Then one day something happens. A different thought enters his mind, and suddenly there is a change in his usual pattern of destructive self talk. It's like a light has been switched on and he is beginning to see things differently.

The fear of not being 'enough', of living his life feeling unlovable and lonely, begins to feel heavy. He is faced with the choice of 'live' or 'die'. He realises that he can start to change his perception, or continue to live miserably at the mercy of influences he believes are beyond his control.

'Living' means, changing the programmes that have been running his life.

'Living' means, making different choices.

'Living' means, letting go of the lies that had convinced him he was eternally flawed.

He begins to see that his allegiance to things outside of himself as the source of his love has been misplaced. He had put such faith in them, but they always let him down!

Now he begins to entertain the possibility of his inherent goodness, his perfect innocence, and his worthiness of being loved no matter what. The masks he wears are feeling oppressive and uncomfortable. He starts to understand that **he** is the creator of his life; that if he takes responsibility for this and makes different choices, he will live a different outcome!

He intentionally rewrites the CD in his mind. Using conscious awareness, he begins to change the faulty programming in the unconscious mind. He notices that it's becoming easier to say 'no!' to the addictive behaviours.

Allowing himself to sit consciously in the once-overwhelming feelings of isolation and abandonment, he discovers that the fear he used to believe in, no longer has power over him. He stays present with his breath as his body inhales and exhales, and like waves upon the shore, the feelings simply wash over him before they melt away. He remains gentle, strong and unbeaten.

One day, he sits peacefully on his own and reflects on how comfortable he has become with his own company. It occurs to him that he no longer tries to fill the emptiness that used to threaten to devour him when he was a younger man.

He walks to the mirror and observes the face that looks back at him. The greying hair and facial lines feel strangely comforting. He feels the warmth in his heart embrace his reflection and he starts to smile. Suddenly, a 'knowing' arises from somewhere deep within his heart and spreads throughout his body and into every cell. He knows now without question, that he has finally turned loneliness into solitude.

His mind goes back to the clear canvas at his birth. He remembers the wounding and the pain he grew up with as a child; the anger of his father, the fights his parents used to have, the nights he spent with his hands over his ears trying not to hear.

He reflects on the dissolute fear of his out-of-control adolescence, and the ensuing pain of love gone wrong, as his relationships with girls reinforced his negative self-worth. He thinks about the alcohol he used to abuse to suppress the fear, until that moment during his midlife crisis when he realised he had a choice of living or dying.

As he looks at his reflection in the mirror, he sees other faces looking back at him and he begins to laugh a deep, hearty, belly laugh! The feeling of LOVE that embraces him now embraces them all. He feels such gratitude for being able to unconditionally love these people from his past: his father and mother, his older brother, the kids at school, his friend and partner in alcoholic crime, the women he blamed for the broken relationships…and the one he believed had broken his heart.

He knows that he would have experienced none of it had he decided to laugh at the lies of his imperfection…but neither would he be feeling the richness of a life well-lived. He feels gratitude for all the gifts along the way, for the choices and changes he made as he grew through adulthood, and for the help of an unseen power who called to him constantly. He reflects on how long it took for that 'little boy' to take his hands away from his ears before he could finally hear and feel the unconditional voice of Truth and LOVE.

His experience takes on a transcendental quality. He feels peace, he feels joy, he feels freedom, and he knows that the rest of his life will be the gift he has given himself.

Hand to Mouth

I
The sun beats down on the African plains. The drought has been long and the parched earth looks like an alien wasteland. She clutches her dying baby to her shrunken breast, resting him against skeletal ribs. Flies crawl like parasites all over their bodies; no strength, or reason, to brush them away.

She looks to the sky, certain that no rain will come to save her child.

A plane flies overhead like a silent missile; an optical illusion out of place in the backdrop of this ghostly valley of death.

II
'Good afternoon Ladies and Gentleman. The cabin crew will now begin moving through the plane with lunch and beverages. Please check the menu in the seat-pocket in front of you.'

'Sir, which meal would you like? The beef stew? Certainly, enjoy.'

'Hello madam, what beverage would you like? We have juice, water, wine or soft drink; white wine? And your son ... lemonade? Here you are. I trust you are enjoying the flight!'

III
Large trucks bring food and water into the refugee camp. Millions of men, women and children have crossed the borders, fleeing from the wars and famine in their own countries, to safety and security in North Eastern Kenya.

A group of people stand around a large rectangular hole dug deep in the unrelenting red earth. Wrapped bodies are gently lowered into their final resting place, the soil of hope and safety.

A man stands in anguished disbelief as he helps to lower her body. He can still see the look of hopeless despair on her face as she holds their baby's lifeless form for the last time. Four days after arriving at the camp, his wife's broken and emaciated body breathed its last breath.

IV

'What's that on the news? Bloody boat people! Get back to where you come from! What? Yeah, I'll have a beer.

I'm sick of these bloody refugees trying to cheat their way into our country! It's bad enough that they get in through the regular channels. Did you know that they get given housing, money and cars? Given! We're not that privileged! We have to work for our money and our hard earned tax dollars get given to them! Shoot the people smugglers and send the refugees back to their own countries! Make me Prime Minister, I'll bloody do it!'

V

The American tanks roll periodically through the city and the rebel insurgents try to ward them off with their bombs. Grabbing her two children, she ducks under the table and gently sobs in despair. The sound of gunfire has become so commonplace these days, and yet she knows she will never get used to it.

The horror of yesterday comes flooding back to her mind. Her husband knew of a man who could help them get away to safety. There is a refugee camp well-across the border; he has to do something to save his family! Their city is crumbling daily; food is getting harder to find and it is getting harder to stay alive.

She watched him walk furtively up the street towards the building where this man was living. Suddenly, the all-too familiar crack of a firing gun resounded and she saw her husband drop heavily to the ground. She screamed at him as she banged upon the closed window pane. 'Get up! Please get up! You have to come back!' He didn't move.

Under the table her youngest child starts to cry. She holds him tighter, remembering the life they used to enjoy. 'Whose fight is this?' she asks in her mind. 'Things have become so crazy! I feel like an insect trapped in a spider's web and I don't know what to do. Is this the day I die?'

VI

'Billy, it's time to turn your computer off. I want you to get ready for dinner now.'

'Oh mum. I'm playing Clash of the Titans and I'm nearly at the end of the level. In a few minutes I'll have killed them all. Can't I keep going? Dad's not home yet!'

VII

One day, her father stopped breathing. They said it was the mosquitoes. She lives with her mother, two brothers, her mother's parents, her uncle and three cousins in the slums of Mumbai. It's a crowded city of extremes. Standing on the high road, she can look over to the city where the rich people live. She and her older brother go there to beg rupees.

There are millions of people living in these slums. A lot have come from the country looking for a better life. Every day she and her family pick over the rubbish looking for something useful. Many of their clothes come from this rubbish. Sometimes they find things to sell or swap.

Her grandfather, her uncle and her cousins make pottery to sell. They make just enough money to pay rent on a single-room house.

VIII

A young girl kneels beside her bed, her palms pressed together.

'Dear God. I know that you love us. How can you get other people to know how much you love them? I think many have forgotten; there seems to be so many unhappy people in the world.

I see them on Television; there are people starving and children dying.

I see them in the news; there are soldiers killing, and politicians blaming,

I see them on the streets in my city, and in fancy cars.

No one seems to be hearing you.

There is enough in the world for everybody. Please help them to trust and to open up their hearts, so we can have a happy world with happy people and happy children?

Amen.'

Cough in your Elbow

I'm going to be the teacher and you can be the students. Sit down and listen to what I have to say.

One upon a time when I was young, we were taught to put our hand across our mouth when we had to cough or sneeze. My mum would say 'Hand for your mouth,' to remind us when we forgot. Where I lived, it was a small town and people didn't crowd around in public transport or shopping centres. We didn't even have shopping centres like we do today.

These days, some people cough and sneeze as they are sitting or standing unmasked on public transport, or walking around shopping centres and supermarkets without even covering their mouths, but most people put their hand over their mouth to stop the germs blowing out onto other people.

Now, what happens to the germs that are on the hands of the coughers and the sneezers?

If they touch nothing and wash their hands straight away, or rub antibacterial gel on their hands, the germs are pretty much deleted.

Think back to times when you have been out in public and seen people cough and sneeze into their hands? What did they do with their hands afterwards?

Yes, they touched the hand rails and buttons on the bus. They touched seats and handles on the train. They picked up items off the supermarket shelf and put them back. They used their germy fingers to key in their pin number at the bank machines and the supermarket checkouts. They even served your mum and dad their takeaway coffee that they ordered at the café. You've probably seen a lot of other situations as well, but that will do for now.

Now, I don't know about you, but since Covid rocked up and became our latest global catastrophe, I have also noticed some people of all ages cleaning their nose with their fingers instead of using a tissue or a handkerchief. They have probably done that for years and I hadn't really noticed?

I googled 'Cough in your Elbow' yesterday, and was very surprised at the first thing that came up. Apparently, some kids in America were successfully taught to cough in their elbows as early as late last century.

With Covid-19, the Australian Government was talking about Coughing in the Elbow, and teaching children at school to do this. Unfortunately some people are very slow learners and need help, don't they. Having a compulsory lesson on correct coughing procedures could be an excellent idea. It could be compulsory for every person in Australia to study the lesson and sit an exam afterwards. If they fail, they could have a private teacher help them to succeed and pass their exam. After all, we have to pass the driver's test before we can get our Drivers Licence, don't we?

Maybe this 'cough in your elbow' needs to be part of a language curriculum across all cultures as well. We are an increasingly global community with people migrating, travelling, etc. In many cultures it is considered a positive and essential trait to be a sharing, caring person with family, friends, and even strangers. But there really are some things we need to be selfish about.

Humanity needs to be responsible if we genuinely do care about our family and our friends. We need to train ourselves to stop spreading our germs.

Thank goodness for our elbows!!!

Ok class, what suggestions do you have?

Shock Treatment

Henricus Gerard Cornelus Bruens was born in Groningen, Holland, on Saturday 2 June 1928. Groningen is in the far north of Holland and at this time the world was in between wars.

His mother, Johanna Maria, was the daughter of a Dutch merchant. His father, Cornelus Bruens, was the son of a Sergeant in the Dutch army. In order to advance his military position, Mr Bruens moved his family to Den Hague, the Dutch capital on the Midwest coast, where he attended Army College. On graduating and receiving a new post, he moved them again, this time to Ede, an army town in the middle of Holland.

In WW1, Holland was a neutral country. They also declared neutrality in WW2, but Hitler had another idea, and invaded Holland on 10 May 1940. What followed is known as the Five-Day War, at the end of which a large part of Holland had become German occupied.

On 14 May, due to a miscommunication between German negotiators and their Luftwaffe, German planes began bombing Rotterdam. People in surrounding towns were digging holes in the ground to jump into, in the possible event of a bomb landing close by. Henk (Henricus), nearly twelve by now, was wandering up and down chatting to his neighbours, completely disinterested in digging a safety net for himself. He stopped to have another talk with the elderly neighbour who lived next door, and who was studiously digging a deep hole, when suddenly they heard the frightening sound of German bombs. 'Godtverdomme,' panicked the neighbour as he suddenly experienced a cardiovascular workout of the stressful kind! Thinking a bomb had fallen into his hole with him, he thankfully discovered it was only a terrified Henk!

Rubber was a resource that the Germans took from many sources, including the tyres off bikes. Henk loved exploring on his pushbike, and used to ride around on his rubber-less rims, much to the mirth of the German soldiers. By now, Mr Bruens had risen to a high rank in the Dutch army. Four German officers moved into the Bruens' house and lived with them. The German military had a habit of helping themselves to whatever they required, now a common practice in Holland. One day they took nearly all the blankets in the house, and sent them to their army supplies. This was the last straw! Incensed at the occupation, Henk rode to the army stores, managed to recover some of the blankets and rode away under gunfire; the soldiers didn't care who they shot!

The German Army was sending a lot of food out of Holland, and used rationing to control the people. Supplies became limited, and people would walk several kilometres to the farms with valuables to trade. Mrs Bruens sent Henk to exchange expensive jewellery for milk and eggs. On the way back he would often dream of eating a dozen eggs all by himself! Once as an adult, he attempted to realise this wartime dream, but could only manage to eat six!

One day, the townspeople were told by the German occupiers that they could go to the potato farm and pick potatoes. What a boon! Off they went sacks in hand, digging, filling, digging, and dragging. Mrs Bruens sent Henk to the farm to get their share. Curious Henk, however, had a better idea. He decided to go off and watch the German planes all day. Planes were his passion, and he would later join the Dutch air force to serve his compulsory military training.

Suddenly he became aware that the light was beginning to fade, and realised he hadn't filled his sack. Henk raced to the potato farm; there was no one else there. Scurrying along the surface, he picked up the rejects that sat on top of the scrambled earth, and hurried home with his sack of meagre offerings. When he arrived and his father saw what he had brought home, Henk got yet another hiding. The next day they learnt that the Germans had confiscated everyone's sack at the gate, and the Bruens family were the only ones with potatoes.

In 1944, the German-occupied part of Holland entered the Hongerwinter ('Hungerwinter'). Food was severely rationed, butter stocks had disappeared, bread, cheese and vegetable oils had all but disappeared, and meat coupons became worthless. The Germans had destroyed docks and bridges to slow down the advancing allies. Coupled with an unusually cold winter and frozen canals, food supplies were greatly affected. People were starving to death, and many stole to stay alive.

Holland was a literate and developed country, and good medical records were taken throughout the famine, which have subsequently served to be an invaluable scientific resource on the effects of malnutrition.

Henk immigrated to New Zealand in 1954. Like all immigrants of the time, his papers referred to him as an 'alien'. He chose New Zealand over South Africa, thinking 'Palm trees, Hula girls …' and arrived in Wellington by ship, on what he came to know as a typical wet and windy, Wellington day! He decided to be known by his middle name, Gerard, not fancying nicknames of 'Hanky Panky', or 'Corny'. Ironically, he often got called 'Jerry'.

When Gerard met Margaret Lister, he knew she was the one. After knowing her for only three weeks, he took her to his friend's place for dinner and said, 'Watch how Anneke makes the Dutch gravy because you'll be doing that.'

It was 9 February 1958 when I first met Gerard Bruens. We were at the Lower Hutt hospital, and he came racing in to hold me immediately after I was born. As his eldest daughter, I experienced the inadvertent effects of my father's family and wartime trauma. He tried very hard to raise his three children differently from his own upbringing. Becoming a parent myself, I discovered how unconscious behavioural patterns can sneak through into daily life.

It was thought that the Parkinson's my father developed nineteen years later was due to wartime malnutrition. Yet, even during the later years of the early onset dementia which followed, I could still see a spark of his unique sense of humour. He died aged fifty-seven.

Why I don't want to be Prime Minister

Politics was always spelled with a capital 'P' when I was growing up. My mother was a staunch Labour supporter and used to be a member of our local electorate Labour party. My father, God rest his soul, was a Social Credit party supporter for many years. His liberation came in the mid 1970s when a family friend became Secretary of the local chapter of the newly-formed Values Party, the first party in New Zealand politics to raise the issue of the environment.

I was a senior at high school during this momentous time and, as one might expect with such politically focused parents, my own interest in politics was very keen. I joined the Values party with my father and we used to attend meetings and activities together. By 1990, the party had gone through big changes and merged with other social change groups to form the Green party of Aotearoa, New Zealand.

In my early twenties, I pleased my mother by enrolling in Political Science at Victoria University. I'm sure she thought 'Eureka! Her soul is saved.' Salvation, however, was short-lived. Halfway through the course, I left New Zealand to attend a four week Transcendental Meditation retreat in Kashmir, Northern India. My adventures then took me to England for my 'OE' (overseas experience), and I stayed abroad for two and a half years.

There is one thing that stood out for me in the Political Science course. I remember being told that many a young bright-eyed and enthusiastic person had joined politics with a view to make a difference, only to discover the weight and restriction of the party line. In order to survive in politics they were called to align with the political machine, which could mean letting go of one's passion and principles. While this change of allegiance may appear easy for some, there were others who found the cost of giving up their vision and integrity too great, and chose to leave politics, certainly at the party level.

Around this time, I began to realise that any difference I was going to make would be with a spiritual focus, and I started to shift my allegiance from trying to change the world through politics, to changing my life from within. Over time I would come to understand that any change in the world was going to come from me changing my mind about how I saw the world and how I felt about myself. This change in direction did not preclude me from keeping an eye on the political scene and casting my vote each election, or even having a political opinion or two! It did, however, steer me away from the seduction of politics and any mild fantasies I had about becoming more deeply involved with the political machine.

While I was in England I knew little of the political situation back in the mother country, except for the occasional titbit my mother sent me. In 1983 the global news was rife with the proposed deployment of cruise missiles. I noticed posters advertising a CND (Campaign against Nuclear Deployment) March in London for the 22 October. My husband (at the time) was not at all happy with my decision, especially as I was newly pregnant, but I was passionate about the anti-nuclear stand and marched with an estimated 200,000 other anti-nuclear Passionates. Ah, the beating drums of revolution!

The general consensus favoured Germany as being the nation who would stand up and say 'No' to nuclear power. In 1984, the year after I returned to New Zealand, it was my own country under the leadership of David Lange and the newly-elected Labour party, who dared to stand up and say 'No' to nuclear power, including nuclear-powered and nuclear armed ships. Of course America was none too pleased at this rebellious attitude from a country whose population at the time was less than four million people and an estimated population of sixty-four million sheep, but neither were the majority of New Zealanders pleased at the thought of US nuclear-powered submarines gracing their hallowed waters!

Whilst in power, there were some unpopular decisions made by the Labour Party and their finance minister, Roger Douglas. His answer for New Zealand came to be known as 'Rogernomics' and his deregulatory policies alienated many of Labour's traditional supporters. People were losing jobs left, right and centre, and faithful party supporters were left wondering how the Right mutation of their Left Labour Party had occurred.

History shows us that you can't please everybody all of the time and whoever the ruling party is (elected or otherwise), is never popular with all of their constituents. After a term in office, Lange had seen the results of Rogernomics and realised how misaligned they were with his own values and vision. After being elected to office for a second term and some failed reprisals, Lange resigned.

It is my belief that David Lange never forgave himself for allowing Rogernomics to sacrifice the country he had vowed to save. In hindsight, Rogernomics was part of the global shift to a more deeply entrenched free market economy.

Over the years in Australasia I have seen many ministers of politics come and go. I have seen politicians with integrity, politicians who lie, politicians who change the rules you voted them in on like a sleight-of-hand magician, politicians who were overpowered by 'higher powers,' politicians who are in it for themselves and their retirement, and politicians who truly thought they could make a difference.

When John Howard gave his election defeat speech on the eve of the 2007 election, I learnt something valuable. Here was a man that many, including myself, had ruthlessly judged. What I heard that night, were the words of someone who truly believed in what he was doing, someone who had a vision for his country and had acted accordingly. It occurred to me in that moment that, love them or hate them, all leaders do have a vision and I discovered a new respect for their intentions, even though our visions may greatly differ.

People can be quick to change loyalties if you let them down, and they can crucify you when you fail to deliver. Like a love affair, as we are seeing with politicians in the current Australian Labour Party (2012), do the wrong thing, betray the people's expectations, and the relationship is over. Looking at the macrocosmic and very public growth-edge that politicians, and especially Prime ministers, are faced with, I am grateful never to have had political leadership desires. Humiliation and persecution in my small life have been enough to deal with. To experience it on such a national and international scale, I can't imagine how I would have coped.

Once upon a time in those early years of my invincible youth, the illusion of being able to make a political and social difference in 'the world,' seemed palpable. That feeling of unified purpose, joining together as a united and creative force to improve people's lives, the planet's, and my own, was briefly and naively intoxicating. Decades later, having witnessed many short-lived and unsuccessful attempts by political parties to govern effectively, I wonder what politics really is all about. Like that great existential question: 'What is the meaning of life?' I question 'What is the meaning of being a politician?' observing that it no longer appears to arise from an altruistic desire to truly improve anyone's life outside of their own.

Rough Justice

Once upon a time politics was an occupation for people who felt a calling, people who cared about their fellow man and wanted to make a difference in their lives through national and regional governance … or was it?

When I was a young naive, I trusted those in authority. I trusted politicians and I believed them when they told me that they had my best interests at heart. I hadn't yet read of ancient civilisations and the relationship between politics and power, religion and politics, royalty and corruption.

Politicians like George Washington and Franklin Roosevelt were recorded in school history books with affirmation. Our Australasian politicians of old were written about in non-emotive, positive representation, and I assumed that, like me, politicians were ultimately honest, trustworthy individuals who cared about the physical, psychological, and spiritual well-being of their country's inhabitants.

Moving forward into the twenty first century and 'Politics' has become a dirty word in our collective and evolving society.

In the *Macquarie Concise Dictionary*, politics means:

1. The science or art of political government.
6. The use of underhand or unscrupulous methods of obtaining power or advancement in an organisation.

I look at politics today and wonder what motivates a person to run for office? Do they need to have strengths like 'manipulative, devious and unscrupulous' in their resumes? Do they require a strong quest for power in order to reach the selection process?

To be fair, there are certainly some individuals within politics who appear to have a caring vision and a degree of integrity. I wonder how much of this is forfeited when joining a political party and swapping one's allegiance from 'other' to 'self-interest and retirement'?

The success of an incoming government appears to include its ability to stand firm in the firing line of opposition hopefuls and arrows of discreditation and vitriol, whilst aiming their own arsenals at 'the enemy' and standing victorious within the public vote. It is difficult to imagine, however, how anyone can effectively get on with the job they were hired to do when they are on high alert and in constant damage control.

Consider for a moment the political election process as a job interview. Who do you know goes to a job interview and spends their time pointing their finger at the other applicants, making snide and disrespectful comments about them in the hope that their own application will be greatly enhanced and placed at the top of the list? What sort of employer demands strength of character from the staff that represents their company such as:

1. Must be able to win arguments with schoolyard bullies and deceive the teachers as to who started the trouble in the first place.
2. Must be able to myopically hold firm to your own values and avoid supporting the opposition to find workable solutions for the good of the whole.

Job interviews, with which I am familiar, are opportunities to present *yourself*, and tell the prospective employer why *you* are the person for the job and what *you* can bring to the role.

I question what is in the collective psyche of 'we the voting public,' that supports and encourages the constant denigration of opposition political parties? What does this tell us about ourselves and our society if this is the sort of political—and social—behaviour that we are continuously co-creating?

For several years now, I have had a belief that the state of consciousness of the politicians is a direct reflection of the state of consciousness of the people whom they govern. If we the people want more enlightened politicians in power, then surely we the people have to become more enlightened ourselves.

The *Australian Pocket Oxford Dictionary* defines enlightenment as 'act or instance of enlightening or state of being enlightened.'

The *Collins Cobuild Advanced Learner's Dictionary* says enlightenment is 'a final spiritual state in which everything is understood and there is no more suffering or desire. ... *a sense of deep peace and spiritual enlightenment.*'

History speaks of the 'Enlightenment' or 'The Age of Enlightenment (Age of Reason)' of late 17th century Europe and the American colonies. The purpose of this cultural movement of intellectuals was to reform society using reason and science instead of tradition, faith, superstition, and revelation.

Knowledge can indeed be a useful force to empower change because if we always do the same thing then we will always get the same result, and the status quo in a constantly changing universe has to eventually blow apart.

In the Age of Reason, intellectuals and science have become our god and maker, and yet something intrinsic has been lost.

If like attracts like, and we consider that politics is another example of a microcosm of the macrocosm, then what changes do we as the individuals in society need to make within ourselves, in order to create a different experience in our world? New science is informing us that we are what we think, and that if we want a different outcome in our experience, we have to change our minds. Perhaps it is time to accept responsibility for the lives we are 'thinking' into existence, and truly discover the 'spiritual light' meaning of enlightenment?

What sort of political environment would you like to see in your country?

What sort of society would you like to see being governed?

What sort of global nation do you truly want to be a part of?

If enough of us are ready for a real revolution in politics, then maybe it is time we found a new name for the role of political governance?

Perhaps we could find a word or a term that describes qualities of a positive function with authenticity, trustworthiness, and a genuine passion to support people to be the best that they can be; to help them shine through encouragement and unconditional acceptance, and with a clear and unified vision, knowing that we are all ONE and what I do to another I do unto myself.

If we are what we think, then maybe it is time to accept that we are all worthy individuals at heart, and that we **can** create a safe, happy, and peaceful world to live in.

The Dance of Spring

The circular shift through the seasonal clock sounds the promise of another change. Winter's coat has lain solid across the land like a protective parent holding fast their sleeping child. As the earth shifts direction in its eternal dance with the sun, one land awakens to the elation of the joys of spring, while another settles down to the long protective embrace of winter.

The warming climate stirs creatures big and small. Eyes are opening, bodies stretch, and mouths yawn as they awaken from their hibernating slumbers. Rumbling tummies urge them forward, persuading them to leave winter's dreams behind. Whiskers poke out of nooks and crannies like antennae searching for contact.

As the ground thaws, green shoots break through the surface with ever-increasing momentum. Vibrant explosions of colour emerge rapturously in the morning light. Blossoms decorate once-naked trees, waiting resplendently for the bees to partner them in their spring courtship and dance of devotion.

Nature's magicians are working overtime in the elemental kingdom. The dance of spring is a time of joy and awakening, of promise and anticipation, of new life and new potential.

The changing air buzzes with the excitement of newly hatched insects as they take their place in spring's epic production.

The relationship between nature and beast is renewed in this cycle. Friends and foe gather round watering holes, eagerly hydrating their once-dormant bodies. The food chain re-establishes its natural order. Vegetarians feast sumptuously on growing grass and new spring greens while their carnivorous brothers, stalk stealthily, resuming their version of the dance of life, and death!

High above them, birds nest and eggs crack. The forest fills with the sound of newborn chicks, and flitting parents eagerly tending to their young.

All of a sudden, the once sleepy land is moving with emergent life, like a dance floor at a discotheque.

The shortest day has long passed, and as winter's thaw has given way to this dance of spring, summer's symphony calls them on to the longest day when the circular shift of the seasonal clock will sound the promise of yet another change, and the cycle of life continues.

Feel the Burn

Once upon a time, when I was ten years old, I went for a ride on the neighbour's horse. The neighbours lived two doors up from us and kept their horse on some farmland about a kilometre up the Awanui Strait. The area in which we lived was residential with no room to keep anything bigger than dogs and kids.

Andrew was a couple of years older than me, and Robbie, well … he seemed a lot smaller than us; after all he was only eight. Sometimes the horse came round to the house, but the boys, especially Andrew, often rode it at the farm and at pony club.

Like many young girls, I had dreams of being a ballerina … and a horse rider! My short career with ballet hadn't started at this stage and I would find myself dreaming of sometimes one, and sometimes the other.

One day, I was invited to go with the boys to the farm and ride their horse. I thought I had died and gone to heaven! Luckily for me, my mother said 'yes', and the boys' mother drove us out to the farm.

Now, you have to understand, I was a seasoned horse rider. I had ridden in my dreams and could feel it in my bones, so when Andrew said I could ride the horse, I didn't hesitate. I climbed up into the saddle, settled in, and started moving gently up the track on the back of the horse. We were all quite young and this was Kaitaia, New Zealand, not Texas, USA, so as you might expect, the horse was old and dependable; lost its balls, you could say, although there is a proper name for that!

The horse and I moved slowly along the track towards the fence at the end. Once we reached the fence, I turned the horse around and we started heading back along the track. As we walked along, I found myself transported into another time. What joy, what freedom.

The large, bright warm sun shone down onto my bare brown arms. Long black hair fell around my bare chest and the long flat plains spread out on either side of a worn path that seemed to stretch ahead forever. As my horse and I moved together in a unified harmony, a black crow flew overhead, silhouetted against a deep blue sky, and let me know by its very presence that I was travelling in the right direction. All seemed well in my world.

Suddenly a blood curdling yell resounded across the Lakota Sioux plains and the horse jumped in fright. Its powerful contracting hindquarter muscles drew its body backwards as it poised itself momentarily in that space between fright and flight, then off it bolted across the plains, its powerful legs galloping swiftly forward like a war horse thundering in battle.

As my trusty steed sped away as if his life depended on it—as surely he believed it did—I returned to present time to find myself lying face down on my right arm in a puddle of water, one of the many puddles resting that day on the rough track of exposed stones and dirt.

The grey sky watched as the two boys came running from the barn which stood back from the track to the right of where I had been so unceremoniously dumped. Laughing, they ran over to see what had happened. My clothes felt damp as I got up from the ground and as I grabbed my wet and grit-covered wrist, I could feel the burn!

Mrs Bennie—bless her soul—drove us to the doctor so that my painful wrist could be assessed. It was official. I was now an initiate of the 'Order of the Broken Bones,' and walked out of the surgery with a plaster cast around my right wrist and forearm.

Fortunately I had a full recovery after developing a little ambidexterity, and using my left hand until my 'write' hand was strong enough for those scholastic necessities such as the written word.

Andrew Bennie went on to successfully represent New Zealand in the Equestrian Events at the Olympic Games, and has continued to live his Equestrian passion.

The Lawn Chair

The new spring sun shone warmly in the clear blue sky. Clouds had dominated much of winter and to now look up into a cloudless sky, many a heart and mood was lifted.

The sudden laugh of a large kookaburra broke the silent ambience as it sat momentarily on the fence next door. It looked around then turned its head toward the reserve. After another hearty laugh, the kookaburra flew off toward the trees and disappeared from view.

It was another Sunday afternoon with the usual comings and goings at the nursing home. Bill sat heavily in one of the white lawn chairs that had been placed in the beautifully kept garden so that people could come outside and enjoy the warming spring weather. 'Got to get your dose of Vitamin D,' said the nurse cheerily as she marched Bill—slowly—down the corridor and out through the back door.

Bill gazed steadily at the new spring flowers. Rings of jonquils and daffodils stood to attention, mimicking the colour of the sun with their bright yellow petals. Along the outsides, and in gentle contrast, hung the white bells of snowdrops, looking delicately graceful surrounded by the dark green of their stalks and leaves.

Suddenly he noticed the lavish palette of colourful freesias. Once upon a time he could smell the rich and sensual fragrance of these beautiful flowers. The plain ones were his wife's favourite. She used to pick a bunch every few days when they were in season, and place them on the lounge mantelpiece. 'Smell these, Bill,' Sally would say as she brought them inside from the garden.

They first met when she was eighteen years old. He was at a local dance and in she walked with his friend's sister. Bill thought Sally was the most beautiful thing he had ever seen and he knew he wanted to marry her even then.

Some people fit like gloves, and that's how it was with Bill and Sally. They had had a wonderful life together. Bill used to love coming home from work to the smells of dinner cooking. Sally would always greet him with a smile and a kiss, except for those times when she was sick, or very pregnant. Even at the end of the week when Bill was tired, one look at her smiling face would settle his heart and he would sigh with relief, and Thank God that she was married to him.

Bill and Sally had been graced with two children, a girl and a boy. Mary and her husband Rick had moved interstate eight months ago and Jonathon, their youngest, was overseas in America. He had started a new job there two years ago, shortly after his fifty fourth birthday and only three months after his mother died.

It was a shock to Jonathon when he got the phone call. Somehow he just expected his mother would live forever. He can still remember that Thursday night. He had gone out to dinner with his two children, not that they were children anymore; Abby was thirty and Johnno was twenty-six!

They were sitting at their favourite Mexican restaurant when his phone rang. 'Johnny,' said his sister. 'I've got some terrible news. You have to come round to Dad's. Mum has had a massive heart attack ... she's dead!'

Johnny's face looked ashen. 'What's wrong, Dad?' asked Abbey.

'It's Nana, she's dead! We have to go straight round to be with Pop!'

Bill took a deep sigh as he reflected over the last four years since he had celebrated his eightieth birthday. What a great night that was. He certainly hadn't expected to lose his sister to cancer the following year, and the love of his life a year after that. It was traumatic enough when his parents died but that was to be expected, he thought, and besides, his lovely Sally was there to help him get through it. Now she's gone, they're all gone. Mary's moved away because her husband was transferred. Johnny's in the US trying to make another life for himself. Johnno is in London on a working holiday and Abbey—she does try to pop in on the occasions when she and Julian can make it up to the city, bless her.

A small flock of cockatoos landed noisily on the vacant lawn in the reserve and started pecking for tasty morsels. 'Don't encourage them, love,' he used to entreat, but Sally said it was best to be fair to all of God's creatures and used to leave seeds for any bird that wanted to fly into their much loved garden. Bill would have preferred to shoot the ratbags, but that was never going to be allowed!

After Sally died, he'd had a stroke. He never thought she would go first; she was so kind and so good. She was the rock that kept him anchored. Now he felt lost like a rudderless boat floating in a big sea.

It was four weeks after her funeral when Bill found himself in hospital. He remembered the pain creeping down his arm and remembered hearing his neighbour shouting. Next thing he's in an ambulance speeding along the road with sirens blaring. An ironic touch of déjà vu, he thought, and hoped he wouldn't make it to the hospital alive.

'Bill, it's time to come inside for afternoon tea,' said the nurse as she walked over to where he was sitting. She helped him to his feet and they slowly walked back to his room. He never regained the full use of his left arm or left leg, and always needed help to get anywhere of any distance.

Back in his room Bill sat down onerously in his armchair and waited for the afternoon trolley to do its rounds. He slowly but surely began to relax, and with a deep sigh of relief, Bill closed his eyes. After a few moments they suddenly sprang open and he looked down at his left hand; he thought he could feel someone stroking it.

'Bill, can you see me?'

'Sally? Is that really you?' exclaimed a surprised Bill.

He laid his head back against the chair and his lungs took a slow, deep breath. Suddenly, he was aware that he could see his parents and his sister standing in front of him, and most of all he could see his beloved Sally snuggled next to him holding his hand.

Bill's heart started to swell so much that he thought it was going to explode. Gradually, his whole body exhaled and his face beamed the most radiant smile you ever did see. In his mind, Bill was hugging his family and his beloved Sally. Then hand in hand, they left the nursing home and walked off together.

When Carla arrived with the afternoon tea trolley, Bill's slumped body was still and his eyes were closed, but his face was still smiling.

The Time Traveller

'What's that you're reading, Jo?'

'*Through Time into Healing*, by Dr Brian Weiss.'

'Mmmm, doesn't look much like a medical book to me!'

'It's far better reading than any medical book, Sandy. He's a psychiatrist who does past life regressions.'

'A what? Crikey, you and your weird interests. Next you'll be telling me you BELIEVE in that reincarnation stuff!'

'Well, yes, as a matter of fact I do. It's a bit hard not to when you've actually experienced it.'

'Right … whatever,' laughed Sandy. 'Keep taking your medication, Jo. I'm off. My lunchtime is nearly over and I've got to detour to the ladies room.'

'O.K. Sandy, see you later. Enjoy your afternoon.'

Jo went back to reading, eager to finish another chapter before her lunch break was over and she had to return to work.

Sandy walked off to the ladies thinking about Jo and her choice of reading material. 'Didn't take Jo for a fruit loop,' she thought, 'but I don't know her very well yet; she is a new recruit.'

The next day at morning tea, Sandy saw Jo sitting reading in the staff cafeteria. She got herself a coffee and a biscuit and walked over to sit with Jo.

'What on earth happened to you, Sandy,' said Jo, looking at the sling that was holding Sandy's arm to her shoulder.

'I wish I knew. I had a really weird dream last night and woke up this morning with my shoulder in excruciating pain. How bizarre is that?'

'How fascinating, Sandy. What was your dream about?'

'All I remember is a horse knocking me over and stamping on my shoulder.'

'I'll bet it's a past life memory,' said Jo eagerly. 'I was reading about a woman who had a frozen shoulder. She had tried everything from physiotherapy to massage, and even painkillers, but nothing made a difference. She went to see Dr Weiss out of desperation, and he regressed her to a life as a Roman soldier. Apparently the soldier had his shoulder bone sliced with a sword, which wouldn't have been so bad if he had died straight away, but he lay in excruciating pain and bled to death after two sunsets.'

'So, how would knowing that, help her frozen shoulder?' Sandy had a quizzical look on her face as she tried to understand what Jo was telling her.

'Well, reliving the trauma and knowing the lessons of that lifetime made a huge impact. It released the tension patterns and two days later, the pain completely disappeared, restoring full use of her shoulder.'

'Freaky! Having a session with the doc probably scared it away. Oops, is that the time? Back to work, not that I can do much … I'm off to the medical centre in half an hour. I'll see you later, Jo.'

Sandy put her empty cup into the dishwasher and caught the lift back to the third floor where she worked.

It was Monday lunchtime when the two women saw each other again. Sandy was sitting eating her lunch when Jo walked into the cafeteria.

'Hey Jo, come and sit over here,' called Sandy as she waived her hand to get Jo's attention.

Jo walked over to Sandy's table, noticing there was no longer a sling holding her arm to her shoulder.

'Wow, Sandy,' blurted Jo. 'Have you had a miracle?'

'You won't believe what happened,' said Sandy excitedly. 'On Thursday I went to the medical centre to have my shoulder looked at and while I was waiting, I read the notice board. Well, my eyes were hypnotised by an advert talking about past life regression! I tried to brush it off as nonsense 'cos I didn't believe in that stuff,' so I sat down in the waiting room until I got in to see the doctor. He told me he couldn't understand what was causing my shoulder pain and gave me a script for painkillers plus a referral for physiotherapy.

I remembered the story you told me about the Roman soldier, and on the way past the notice board I had this strong feeling to take down the number. I rang it as soon as I left the medical centre and would you believe it—the woman had just had a cancellation for Friday morning! How weird was THAT?'

'That's fascinating,' said Jo as her eyes lit up. Sounds like a little more than coincidence, eh?'

'I reckon! I told her about my dream when we were talking on the phone. She said that it was very significant, and that she was looking forward to meeting me.'

'So what happened when you went to see her?'

'We talked again about my dream. Then she did some breathing with me. She counted me down into a hypnotic state and told me to go back to the time when the injury to my shoulder first occurred. Well! There I was minding my own business. Actually, I was running away and eloping with a boy that I loved. It was Greece over 2000 years ago. My father in that lifetime was a religious and racist bigot, and I was in love with a Turkish boy. I told my mother what I was about to do. She was really upset, but she had lived with my father for twenty years and knew what he was like. She really wanted me to be happy; unlike she had been all these years in her arranged marriage. She gave me her blessing and nervously told me to hurry before my father came back.

The next day was a beautiful warm, sunny day. We had slept the night under some olive trees and began walking across a field, feeling safe and free and very much in love. Suddenly, along came my father riding very quickly on his horse. I hadn't come home the previous night and he had forcibly gotten out of my mother what my plans were. He was murderously angry, and as soon as it was daybreak, he came looking for us.

My father was riding like he was possessed. As he got closer, he drew his sword as if he was in battle. There was nowhere for us to go. Inevitably he reached us, and drove his sword straight through my love's chest. As my true love's dying body fell to the ground, I dropped down beside him, distraught at what I had just witnessed. Next thing, the horse reared up and my father brought it down on my right shoulder. It trampled me, making a mess of my shoulder, the right side of my head, and the organs on the right side of my body. The coward rode off and left me to die. My mother and uncle found me later that day, and brought me back to the village, but I was too damaged physically, and emotionally. I died three days later.'

'Phew. You must have hit the jackpot seeing this therapist because there's no more sling and your arm seems normal.'

'She said it would probably take three days to completely feel healed again, as it took me three days to die in that lifetime. She was right. I took the sling off on Saturday, but the aching didn't completely stop until twenty minutes ago. Funny thing, I recognised my love in that life time. He was Steven, my first boyfriend. We had been inseparable for three years. Then one day we decided it was over. It was just like a spell had been broken; no painful drama.

'What was the life lesson?'

'Oh yeah; she asked me to look at that after I had died. Apparently, it was to choose love and freedom at any cost, and break free from the pattern of subjugation that I had carried on from a few previous lifetimes. She said that the pattern had completely cleared when my relationship with Steven ended.'

'That's fantastic, Sandy. How interesting. I've nearly finished the book. Would you like to read it after me?'

'You beat me to it, Jo,' replied Sandy laughing. 'I'd love to. I think I've turned into a Time Traveller! What do you reckon?'

'I think you have too, Sandy. I'll bring the book in with me tomorrow and you can tell me all about Steven. I'm off to do some shopping now before I get back to work. Enjoy your new found freedom! See you tomorrow.'

'Thanks heaps, Jo; I couldn't have done it without you. See you tomorrow at morning tea.'

As Jo walked out of the lunch room, Sandy sat back and settled into her chair. She looked at her right shoulder, and thought of the events over the last few days. She shook her head gently and thought, 'Wow, there **is** more to life than what you think you can see,' then she picked up her coffee cup and walked over to the coffee machine for a refill before returning to work for the afternoon.

TEN-MINUTE TOPICS

As most writers know, the creative flow can be instantaneous. Sometimes it can be slow to start, but it will get there in the end.

Occasionally, it appears to be in another dimension completely, and try as you might, nothing legible will traverse the journey from creative mind through pen to blank paper canvas.

Towards the end of the weekly U3A Writing Group we would have a ten-minute topic.

First we were given the title on which to write about, then it was all systems go for the next ten minutes!

The following short works were written with the pressure of the clock ticking!

The Bear is Growling

My God, what is that sound? It can't be a bear growling, can it? I mean, I'm walking through the Blue Mountains in Australia, not the Canadian Rockies or the American forest!

I've heard about panthers, and the yowie, but I'm sure there aren't any of those creatures here in the mountains or I would have read about them in the guide book.

Oh! There it goes again. Why did I decide on such a big walk on my own?

Maybe it's a dingo. Jeez, that would be scary. I can see the headlines now: 'A dingo stole my husband!'

Nope, haven't heard about dingos wandering through Echo Point or cavorting round Minnehaha Falls.

What about the bird life? It's a lot stranger over here than I'm used to in Godzone. Nah, it was more of a growl than a laughing kookaburra or a giggling galah.

Let me sit a minute and calm down.

Oh, there it is again!

Well, what a twit I am. It's not a panther, or a yowie, or a dingo, or a kookaburra, or even a bloody bear.

What a galah I am! It's my sorry, hungry stomach!

Elegant Restraint

She sat poised like a statuette of fine bone china. Her makeup was perfectly applied and not a hair was out of place. The long string of pearls hung heavily from her neck and draped around her body as she sat elegantly waiting for the photographers to finish shooting the stills for the movie promo.

On the road beside them stood the model T Ford that had driven her into the temporary set at Coogee beach.

The sun was warm and the sky was blue. It took all her strength not to be distracted by the gentle sound of the waves caressing the sandy beach.

She could hear the sea birds and the laughing children, and realising she had let her attention wander she brought herself back to the task at hand.

'Can you swing your legs to the other side?' said the director.

This change of position put her in direct visual contact with the alluring water. What purgatory it was to be imprisoned in such elegant restraint on a magical summer's day beside the beach!

After ten more minutes of total compliance, she stood up and said, 'It's a wrap,' and ran down to the beach. She tossed her shoes, accessories and dress onto the sand, and jumped into the velvet water.

Lexicography, Cough, Sigh, Alphabet, Multiply, Lunch, Cats Litter, Batter, Cloth

Mavis let out a big sigh and muttered to herself. 'These bloody crosswords are getting harder and harder!'

She thought about lunch and the batter she made earlier for the fish Bert caught yesterday. 'You loved the fish, didn't you loves,' she said as the two cats jumped off the kitty litter.

Looking back at the crossword book, Mavis started to go through the alphabet but it didn't help. She gave a cough and decided she was beat. Looking at the back of the crossword book she found the answers for the puzzle she was having trouble with.

'Lexicography!' she exclaimed. 'Bloody hell, I don't even know what that means!'

'Lunchtime,' she called out as she put her book away under the cloth and limped into the kitchen. The playful cats nearly got in her way and as much as she loved them, she was grateful that their numbers were not going to multiply.

The Sandman

'There he is again, mummy,' exclaimed Jimmy pointing his finger down the beach.

His mother looked up from the picnic she was laying out for the family and saw the sandman walking along the beach in their direction. She remembered his life story and felt a twinge of sadness that quickly turned into deep compassion.

'Don't point, Jimmy,' she said as she un-wrapped the sandwiches and placed them on a plate next to the fruit cake.

'Mm mmm,' said her husband when he looked at the plate of generously filled egg and mayonnaise sandwiches. They were his favourite; one of those left over relics of childhood that kept his mother's memory alive.

Jenny looked up to see the sandman walking closer along the soft sand. She took a napkin and opened it up. In the middle she placed a slice of fruit cake and two sandwiches, and then she neatly wrapped it up.

'Jimmy, I want you to do something for mummy,' she said as she picked up a banana and handed it to Jimmy with the parcel of cake and sandwiches. 'Please run down the beach to the sandman and give these to him?'

'Sure mummy,' replied Jimmy, and he ran down the beach to the sandman.

'Here, Mister. These are for you from my mum.' Jimmy looked up at the man's vacant eyes. His hands trembled as they took the food, and Jimmy saw a little tear begin to roll down the sandman's left cheek.

Bells and Whistles

He waited on the platform holding tightly to his mother's hand. Suddenly he heard the 'chug, chug' of the steam train and squealed with unbridled excitement. They looked down the tracks and saw the train coming round the bend, and watched it as it slowed down in its approach to the station. Bells clanging and whistles blowing heralded its arrival as it stopped in front of them. Steam blew everywhere and sounds of hissing enveloped the passengers waiting on the platform.

'Mummy, mummy, is this really happening?' said the little boy.

'Yes it is, darling. Daddy's boat has come ashore and we are going to visit him.'

'Thank you,' said his mother as a disembarking passenger held the door open for her and helped the little boy up the steps.

They found their seats and in no time, the sound of bells and whistles could be heard again as the train moved slowly out of the station. This was going to be his best adventure ever!

The Comeback

Lou sat in his armchair looking at the blank television screen. His mind wandered to the victory moment. There he stood inside the ring with the crowd clapping and cheering—cheering for him! The referee had just counted out his opponent who was now staggering to the other side of the boxing ring. Lou's arm was raised like an antenna as he revelled in the crowd's jubilation.

The gold trophy was put in his hands and he kissed it with all his passion. What a fight that was! Who said he was too old to fight?

He looked over at the trophies on his shelf to admire this precious prize, but it was not there. There had been no comeback. There had been no final trophy.

Lou was an old man now and could only live fights in his wandering mind.

Retirement

To retire, or not to retire, that is the question?

Well actually, these days retirement for many seems to be a distant hope.

Once upon a time, we knew where we were going. We could pride ourselves in the longevity of one job of employment and forty years long service was our reward.

These days, if you send in your resume to a prospective employer and you have had only one prior job and you are over fifty years old, they look at you suspiciously and wonder what's wrong with you.

As time goes by, and the economy keeps fluctuating, that pinnacle of freedom after a life of employment well lived, becomes increasingly elusive as the governments of the day keep shifting the finishing line.

It is becoming harder and harder for those in the race to retirement, and some fall by the wayside unable to reach their life's goals.

I wish I could win a few million dollars in Lotto to secure the future of my retirement.

NOTES

INTRODUCTION

'U3A' is a global organisation called University of the Third Age which generally provides classes for people who are fifty years and over. The curriculum is wide ranging and helps to keep the maturing brains stimulated.

'Yellow Brick Road' is a well-known symbol mentioned in the 1939 movie *Wizard of Oz*.

'... two emotions, love and fear.' *A Course in Miracles*, 2nd Edition, 1992, T-13, V. 1, p. 247.

'All healing is essentially the release from fear.' *A Course in Miracles*, 2nd Edition, 1992, T-2.1, V. 1:7, p. 23.

POETRY

Ask me no Questions and I'll Tell you no Lies
Farenheit 9/11 is a 2004 American documentary film that was directed, written by, and starring, filmmaker, director, political commentator and activist, Michael Moore.

My Red Gum Friend
Angophora costata is the name for the Sydney Red Gum tree.

Bullaburra is a town in the Blue Mountains, West Sydney, Australia. In 2013 when I wrote this poem, the meaning I found of the name Bullaburra, was 'clear skies'. Unbeknownst to me at the time, this poem was going to be part of a book. Had I known this in advance, I would have saved the source. Moving ahead ten years, and the Aboriginal meaning of Bullaburra is listed as 'blue sky'. A Wikipedia source states the meaning as 'clear day', so I have chosen to use that translation, <wikipedia.org/wiki/Bullaburra,_New_South_Wales>.

Do me no Favours
Hamlet, a play written by William Shakespeare around 1600, <wikipedia.org/wiki/Hamlet>.

'Peace begins with Me' is a reminder that we all carry emotional pain and negative beliefs. The more of us who embrace and heal our wounds, change our mindsets from negative to positive, and spend more time in the presence of LOVE and True Self-acceptance, the closer we will get to a happy, safe, peaceful life on our global planet.

Pull Your Finger Out
Midas and the Golden Touch is a story from Greek mythology.

Nikola Tesla was a genius inventor who initially started the concept of wireless power.

J. P. Morgan was a wealthy Industrialist and American financier.

Erin Brokovich (2000) is a wonderful movie that raised awareness about industrial pollution in America and the effects it has on people. Fracking happens in Australia also, but some European countries have banned it.

Weeping Tigers
'Woman is awakening' is the female energy within every human. There is an increasing number of men who are softening, healing, and embracing their nurturing abilities.

The Affluent Society
This poem is not anti-Australian. Sadly it is indicative of several countries in the world. After I wrote this poem in 2013, I returned to New Zealand for a visit and saw no difference there.

Boys in Blue
When I wrote this poem in 2012, police cars in NSW, Australia, were often yellow, red, or blue and reminded me of jelly bean lollies. I was driving down the Blue Mountains one day and I noticed a police car parked on the left side with the driver watching traffic. Suddenly, I noticed another police car driving up the road on my right, and the poem started writing in my mind.

I want to say a big **Thank You** to the police. I acknowledge the mental struggles and physical/emotional pain many of you endure. Without your commitment and support, I can't imagine how we would survive.

The Pot of Gold
'Illusion recognised must disappear,' *A Course in Miracles*, 2nd Edition, 1992, W-pl.187.7:1.

My Christmas Wish

The modern version of the 'Serenity Prayer' is very popular. It is based on the original version claimed to be written by Reinhold Niebuhr (1892–1971).

SHORT STORIES

Sitting on the Esky

David Tobin and Theresa West live in Lawson in the Blue Mountains and are two musicians who have made a wonderful contribution to the local music scene.

'Over the Rainbow' is a ballad written by Harold Arlen with lyrics by Yip Harburg, for the 1939 film *The Wizard of Oz*.

Stage Interlude

The voice written in italics is my Higher Self speaking to me.

Romeo is a character from *Romeo and Juliet*, a play written by William Shakespeare around 1594.

Sleeping Beauty, *Robin Hood*, *Prince Charming*, *Rapunzel*, *Cinderella*, and the *Beast*, are all characters in movies by Walt Disney Productions that I grew up with, and like many others, believed to be real interpretations of how our lives would unfold.

I wrote 'First Step' in 1991.

'I'm still getting wet when I go swimming' means that I cannot walk on water like Jesus did and am therefore, still a mere mortal who hasn't reached full enlightenment.

'I'm sorry, I forgive me, I bless me, I love me,' is one of my interpretations of the Ho'oponopono Prayer inspired by Dr Hew Len.

'Nothing real can be threatened. Nothing unreal exists. Herein lies the peace of God,' is a quote from the Introduction in *A Course in Miracles*.

Life of Brian (1979) is a movie by Monty Python.

Turning Loneliness into Solitude

Psychologist Carl Jung (1875–1961) uncovered the 'inner child wounding'.

Dr Bruce Lipton explains Epigenetics in his book *Biology of Belief.*

The meaning of 'partner in alcoholic crime' in this story is simply two people abusing alcohol, and getting drunk every time they catch up.

Shock Treatment
Wikipedia explains the Dutch 'Hungerwinter' that my father experienced in Holland along with many others during the Second World War, <https://en.wikipedia.org/wiki/Dutch_famine_of_1944>.

Why I don't want to be Prime Minister.
David Lange was in office as Prime Minister of NZ for five years from 1984–1989.

'Jean Paul Satre: Existentialism' by Christian J. Onof. *The Internet Encyclopedia of Philosophy*, ISSN 2161-0002, <iep.utm.edu/sartre-ex/>.

Rough Justice
Macquarie Concise Dictionary, 8th Edition, 2020, p. 496.

Australian Pocket Oxford Dictionary, 2019, p. 369.

Collins Cobuild Advanced Learner's Dictionary, 2023 publication, p. 496.

'Age of Enlightenment/Age of reason,' <en.wikipedia.org/wiki/Age_of_Enlightenment>.

Cough in Your Elbow
ABC News explains that coughing in our elbows can reduce the spread of contagions from Colds, Flu's, etc., <abcnews.go.com/Health/ColdandFluNews/story?id=651134&page=1>.

Feel the Burn
Thank you to Andrew Bennie and his family for being such good neighbours.

The Time Traveller
Through Time Into Healing by Dr Brian Weiss, Piatkus Books, 1998 publication, pp. 56–57.

TEN-MINUTE TOPICS

The Bear is Growling
'Echo Point' and 'Minnehaha Falls' are both tourist attractions in Katoomba, Blue Mountains in Greater West Sydney, Australia.

A Galah is a bird that is native to Australia. It is also the term for a 'Fool or silly person,' *Macquarie Best Aussie Slang* by James Lambert, 2008, <http://www.koalanet.com.au/australian-slang.html>.

Lexicography, Cough, Sigh, Alphabet, Multiply, Lunch, Cats Litter, Batter, Cloth

This was a ten-minute topic in which we had to incorporate each of the above words into a story in only ten minutes; quite a creative challenge!!!

www.ingramcontent.com/pod-product-compliance
Lightning Source LLC
Chambersburg PA
CBHW062050290426
44109CB00027B/2784